P9-CNE-786

"Many a child and many a single-parent family will be happier and more comfortable and contented because of the explicitly helpful suggestions offered by Dr. Gardner in this timely book."
—*Louise Bates Ames, M.D.,*
Acting Executive Director,
Gesell Institute of Child Development

"A much needed and highly recommended book for parents, teachers, and mental health professionals as well as children."
—*Irving Berlin, M.D.*
President, American Academy
of Child Psychiatry

"This book is destined to become a classic. It fills a need that never before existed to this extent."
—*Daniel Sugarman, Ph.D.,*
Professor of Psychology,
William Paterson College

PROPERTY OF RIVERWOOD CENTER

Other Bantam Books by Richard A. Gardner, M.D.
Ask your bookseller for the titles you have missed

THE PARENTS BOOK ABOUT DIVORCE
THE BOYS AND GIRLS BOOK ABOUT DIVORCE
THE BOYS AND GIRLS BOOK ABOUT STEPFAMILIES

THE BOYS AND GIRLS BOOK ABOUT ONE-PARENT FAMILIES

Richard A. Gardner, M.D.

*Clinical Professor of
Child Psychiatry
Columbia University,
College of Physicians and
Surgeons*

**Now Distributed By
Creative Therapeutics
155 County Road
Cresskill, New Jersey 07626**

BANTAM BOOKS
TORONTO • NEW YORK • LONDON • SYDNEY • AUCKLAND

THE BOYS AND GIRLS BOOK ABOUT ONE-PARENT FAMILIES
*A Bantam Book / published by arrangement with
G. P. Putnam's Sons*

PRINTING HISTORY
Putnam's edition published December 1978
Special abridged edition of Putnam Book
Bantam edition / June 1983

*Song Title: "Cry." Copyright MCMLI by Shapiro, Bernstein &
Co., Inc. New York, N.Y. 10022. International Copyright Secured.
All Rights Reserved Including Public Performance for Profit.*

All rights reserved.
Copyright © 1978 by Richard A. Gardner, M.D.
Cover art copyright © 1983 by Bantam Books, Inc.
*This book may not be reproduced in whole or in part, by
mimeograph or any other means, without permission.*
*For information address: G. P. Putnam's Sons,
200 Madison Avenue, New York, N.Y. 10016.*

ISBN 0-553-13809-X

Pubished simultaneously in the United States and Canada

*Bantam Books are published by Bantam Books, Inc. Its trade-
mark, consisting of the words "Bantam Books" and the por-
trayal of a rooster, is Registered in U.S. Patent and Trademark
Office and in other countries. Marca Registrada. Bantam
Books, Inc., 666 Fifth Avenue, New York, New York 10103.*

PRINTED IN THE UNITED STATES OF AMERICA

O   9 8 7 6 5 4 3 2

CONTENTS

PART II—LIVING WITH A MOTHER WHO HAS NEVER BEEN MARRIED

PART III—LIVING WITH ONE PARENT AFTER THE OTHER HAS DIED

INTRODUCTION FOR PARENTS

This is a book for children living in one-parent homes. It is for children who live with one parent because of divorce, death or single parenthood.

Growing up in any of these three types of households does not necessarily cause a child to develop psychological difficulties, but the child in such a home runs a greater risk of developing such problems than the child in a two-parent *stable* home. However, the child in a two-parent *unstable* home is more likely to develop psychological disorders than the child in a one-parent stable home. It is not so much the number of parents a child has but their psychological stability that determines the child's psychological health.

This book was written to help children in one-parent homes deal with some of the common problems that are likely to arise. It is designed to be read by children who have reached about the third to fourth grade level of reading comprehension. Younger children (down to about age six) will understand much when read to. Some in this age bracket enjoy reading what they can while parents assist with words they have not yet mastered.

Although this is not a fun book in the traditional sense, it is designed to be attractive to a child. Its lure comes from the fact that the issues discussed in it are of vital interest to children living in one-parent homes. It has been the author's experience that when such issues are presented in the manner used here, children will often become intensely curious. Their interest and absorption is derived from their appreciation that the problems being discussed are the very ones that have been causing them so much concern and even grief. Furthermore, the Lowenheim illustrations have proved to enhance even further children's involvement in the material.

Adolescents can also benefit from this book, though they may exhibit some hesitation at the prospect of reading it. They may consider it to be beneath them because of the fact that it is written at the third to fourth grade level. In addition, the cartoon illustrations may also remind them of books for younger children. The messages provided here, however, are for all ages. Parents will immediately recognize that I am writing for them as well. Accordingly, there is much here that the adolescent can profit from if he or she can be encouraged to overcome that initial balkiness. Observing his or her parent reading the book is probably the best way to help the adolescent overcome these early reservations.

Regardless of the child's age, it is important for parents to keep in mind that this book should not be considered a form of do-it-yourself therapy. Rather, its aim is to *prevent* the development of problems that may (but not necessarily do) result from the one-parent situation by dealing with difficulties at their earliest stages. Its aim also is to alleviate minor problems— those that may respond to guidance and advice. When such problems have become deeply entrenched, however, it is not likely that the kind of information presented here will be very useful. A more extensive form of therapeutic intervention is usually warranted in such situations.

The fundamental premise of this book is that open discussion of pertinent issues is the first and most effective step toward the prevention and alleviation of many kinds of psychological difficulties. All too often, parents are not direct and honest with children regarding many of the special problems that may arise in the one-parent household. The parents usually mean well. They believe that such revelations would be detrimental to the children and cause them more harm than good. I do not agree. More problems arise when important information is withheld than when too much is given. Now, I am not saying that the parent's life should be an open book and that only by telling everything will the child be protected from psychological damage. "Letting it all hang out" can be as detrimental as saying nothing. I am saying only that too many parents err on the side of too much withholding. It is the purpose of this book to help open things up, to reveal what is appropriate and judicious for children to know.

Therefore, this book is not just for the child to read and follow. It is important that the child *and* parent talk about the issues raised in the book as points of departure for meaningful discussion. This may not only serve to alleviate the problems being discussed, but should help to bring parent and child closer. The basic premise of the book is that such open interchanges are the most effective way of resolving the kinds of problems that arise in single-parent homes and of reducing the parent-child estrangement so common in such situations.

No author can expect a reader to agree with everything that he has to say. Accordingly, there may be opinions expressed here with which a parent might disagree. In such cases, I would recommend that the parent reread carefully what I have said to be sure that my position has been clearly understood. If after such rereading the parent is still convinced that I am in error, then the parent will do well to inform the child of his or her disagreement. The child might be given the opportunity to make his or her own decision on the matter (and the older the child the more capable he or she is of doing this). This difference can serve as a point of departure for what might be a useful discussion. Such expression by the parent can also be useful to the child in another way. It communicates to the child that one can have occasional disagreement with someone and yet still basically have respect for most of what that person has to say.

Some passages in this book may stir up feelings not

only in the child, but in the parent as well. This should not be a reason for putting it down. Rather, the opportunity should be seized upon to express such feelings. I am not providing advice here for the child that does not hold for the parents. The book is based on the principle that expression of thoughts and feelings with the appropriate parties can be highly effective in reducing psychological difficulties. So when parents find the book evoking such reactions, they do well to express their thoughts and feelings to their children. Such parents serve as good models for their children.

I would also like to point out that this book was not designed to be read in one sitting. No child (and, in fact, no parent) could be expected to absorb all its contents at once. It is best read in short segments, in order to provide the child the opportunity to become comfortable with advice that may be difficult to comprehend or implement. It is not crucial that it be read in sequence. Some children prefer to scan the table of contents and read those parts that appeal to or are particularly relevant to them. Generally that choice of material is determined by the child's interests and needs.

There are also times when a child will avoid certain sections of the book because they are anxiety provoking, and, when this happens, the child's decision should be respected. However, parents need not fear that any psychological harm will come to the child if such sections are read to the child, or even anxiously read by the child himself or herself. One can depend upon various psychological defense mechanisms to protect the child from any possible untoward reactions from reading such material. Psychological problems are not caused by occasional episodes of anxiety. Rather, they are caused by long-term exposure to ongoing detrimental influences.

I believe this book is best read when the child is relaxed and comfortable. A competing television program or the distracting sounds of other children playing will not provide the proper atmosphere for the child to comprehend and absorb the book's contents. Bedtime has traditionally been the time for children's reading, both alone and with a parent, and if the child is still quite alert, bedtime would be a good time for reading this book. But if the child is sleepy, he or she is not likely to gain much from reading it at that time.

Parents will know that they are using this book successfully by the child's interest in reading it (alone or with the parent) and by the child's receptivity to discussing its messages. Such discussions not only help resolve the problems that may occur in a one-parent household, but deepen the parent-child bond as well.

INTRODUCTION FOR BOYS AND GIRLS

My name is Dr. Richard Gardner. I am a child psychiatrist. Some of you may not know what that is. A child psychiatrist is a doctor who tries to help children who have problems and worries.

Sometimes a psychiatrist can help a child, and sometimes he or she can't. This is because a great deal depends on how much a child tries to help in solving problems. Children who do not work hard at it do not usually help themselves. Those who do often end up having less trouble. The child psychiatrist, then, does not solve your problems for you. Rather, he or she helps you help yourself.

In this book, I try to help children with problems they may have because they are living in a home with only one parent. Most often this comes about when the parents separate and get divorced. Sometimes this happens when a parent dies. And once in a while, it happens because the parent hasn't gotten married. In all of these situations, children are living in a home with only one parent. And special problems can arise in such a home. It doesn't always have to happen that problems come about in such homes, but they often do.

So in this book I try to help children who live in one-parent homes to deal with and solve some of these problems. I say *try* because I cannot be sure I can always help. As I said before, it also depends upon a child's desire to help himself or herself. And I say *some* of the problems because I cannot promise to help with all of them. The most important thing that will decide how many of the problems will be solved is what the boy or girl does to help.

If you read this book carefully and try to follow the advice in it, you are likely to be helped with some, and perhaps a lot, of your problems. If you read it but don't try to follow the advice, you are not likely to change the things that are bothering you.

I would now like to tell you about an old statue of three monkeys. One is covering his mouth, one is covering his eyes, and one is covering his ears. Below them it says, "Speak no evil, see no evil, hear no evil." Evil means bad things. The person who wrote this wanted to warn people not to say bad things, look at bad things, or listen to bad things.

In my opinion, some of this advice is not always very good. Sometimes it's better to speak about, look at, and listen for bad things. If you speak about, look at, and listen for bad things, you may be able to protect yourself in advance from things that can cause you trouble.

Of course, parents of children living in one-parent homes do not usually do things that could be called

evil. But many things do happen in such homes that are bad for children. Children who behave like the monkeys and don't want to speak about, look at, and listen for them are hiding from their troubles. This may make them feel better for a while. But because they aren't doing anything to change things, they aren't going to solve any of their problems. They aren't going to lessen any of their worries. So don't you be like the three monkeys if you want to feel better about the problems you may be having because you live in a one-parent home.

I learned most of the things I talk about in this book from children like yourself, children who live in one-parent homes. They and their parents have come to me for many years to ask my help in solving some of their problems. These people have learned many things from their mistakes. By reading this book, you can learn to avoid many of the mistakes they have made. And of course, it is better to learn from the mistakes of others, because then you don't feel the pain that they did.

This may not be an easy book for many of you to read, and it is not the kind of book that should be read all at once. No child I know could possibly remember all the things I say here after reading the book quickly at one time. The best way to use this book is to read a small amount at a time.

Many children like to read this book along with a parent. When you do this, it's best to stop every once in a while and talk to your parent about what you have just read. Then you can be sure that you have understood it and you can also exchange ideas with your parent. Younger children, who can't read too well, will often find it useful to have a parent read to them.

Some boys and girls find it useful to look at the Table of Contents and read those parts they thing will be of most interest to them. This is a good way to read this book because not every part is going to tell about your problems. Different children have different problems and so may want to read different parts of this book. You may also want to go back to it from time to time, and as you grow older you'll be able to better understand things that you may not have understood when you were younger.

If you read this book carefully and try to do the things that I suggest in it, I think you will find ways to solve many of the problems you may have. In addition, I think that you will feel better about yourself.

Part I

LIVING WITH ONE PARENT
AFTER A DIVORCE

1

SOME IMPORTANT THINGS YOU SHOULD KNOW ABOUT DIVORCE

When one of the parents first moves out of the house, the parents are said to be *separated*. When parents are separated, although living apart, they cannot marry other people. After some time, usually many months or a few years, they get a piece of paper from the court which says that they are *divorced*. Then each one is free to marry someone else if he or she wishes to. Sometimes a divorced parent does marry another person, and sometimes not.

In this part of the book, I will talk about the kinds of things that can happen to you if your parents' marriage breaks up. For each problem, I am going to try and give you advice on what you can do to try to find a solution.

IS DIVORCE ALWAYS BAD FOR CHILDREN?

When parents separate, children most often, but not always, feel sad. Some are so sad that they think that it's the worst thing that will happen to them in their whole life. And they usually wish very hard that their parents would get back together again so that they won't feel so unhappy. But often, the divorce isn't as bad as you might think. I will explain why.

There are mainly three kinds of homes that most children live in.

The first is one in which the parents are happy with each other *most of the time*. Such a home is the best for children to grow up in, but unfortunately, many children are not lucky enough to have such a home.

The second kind of home is one in which the parents are unhappy with each other most of the time, but do *not* get divorced. They may fight a lot or not talk to each other for days and even weeks, yet they still stay together. Unhappily, when boys and girls who grow up in such a home become adults, the only thing they may remember of their childhood is their parents' fighting.

The third kind of home is one in which there is only one parent.

WHICH IS WORSE: AN UNHAPPY HOME OR A DIVORCE?

That is the big question. Which is worse for a child? the two-parent home with a lot of fighting? or the one-parent home that may be more peaceful?

If your parents are unhappy together, you may well be much better off in a one-parent home. The noise and fighting will have finally stopped, and both parents may then be happier. And if the parent who has left the house, but whom you visit, loves you very much and sees you as often as possible, then you are certainly better off than in the home with a lot of fighting.

However, if your parents continue fighting after the separation and the divorce and even try to involve you in their fighting, you are *very* likely to have problems. Later in this part of the book I will give you some advice for such problems.

KNOWING THE REASONS FOR A DIVORCE

Some parents don't tell their children about the main reasons for a separation or divorce. They think that criticisms of each other are bad for children to hear.

I don't agree. No one is perfect. Everyone has at least some faults and parents are no exception. I believe it is important for you to learn what parts of your parents to like and what to dislike so that you will copy only the good parts as you grow up.

Of course, when parents explain the reasons for a divorce, they may still be so angry and upset that they may say things about each other that aren't true. For example, a mother might tell a boy that his father is mean but when the boy visits his father the father is usually very nice to him. He then realizes that his

father isn't mean to him, although it is still possible that he was mean to his mother.

So, it is important for you to hear about your parents' good and bad parts but also to learn to use your own eyes and ears to decide for yourself what you like and what you don't like. The older you get, the better you will be able to do this.

There is also another important reason for learning that all parents have some faults. Children who believe that their parents are perfect may grow up believing that there are other perfect people as well. They then become very disappointed when they find that every person has some faults. They may have trouble getting boy and girl friends as teenagers because they cannot accept faults. Later they may have trouble finding someone to marry because they will settle for nothing less than a perfect person. And they may have trouble

with friends, bosses, and the people they work with because they become angry at anyone who has faults.

So if your parents haven't told you the reasons for their separation or divorce, ask them what they were. Tell them what I have said here about how important it can be. Tell them also about the kinds of problems that can be caused by your not having this information. I hope they will tell you and also answer your questions.

UNDERSTANDING HOW PARENTS CAN STOP LOVING EACH OTHER

Most parents, when they decide to get married, love each other very much. At that time angry, unloving, and hateful feelings are not very common. But they do exist in small amounts, even if the people don't realize it. Even then, when people are most in love, some angry feelings are present. Loving feelings do not exist alone. Angry and even hateful feelings are always mixed in too, even when people love each other enough to marry.

Now, you may be wondering why I say that these angry feelings must always be there, even if only in small amounts. I say this because no one can give us all the things we want, just when we want them. When we don't get what we want, we get angry about it—even if we don't show the anger to others and even if we don't want to admit it to ourselves. When two people love each other very much, they enjoy doing things for each other and giving to each other. Because of this, they get what they want from each other *most of the time*. But they can never satisfy each other *all the time*. There will still be times—even if only once in a while—when one or both will not be getting what he or she wants. Then angry feelings come.

After parents have been married for a while, some of the loving feelings may get less and more angry feelings may come. But when the marriage is a good one, the loving feelings are much stronger than the angry ones. This is not very different from what happens between two children who become friends. At first, they may be very excited about each other. They may want to be with each other most of the time. However, as time goes on they usually find out things about each other that they do not like—things that make each one angry at times at the other. Yet, they may still remain friends, because they have many more friendly and loving feelings than angry ones.

But when the marriage is a bad one, the hateful feelings gradually become stronger than the loving ones. And finally, when a marriage is so unhappy that people separate and divorce, the hateful feelings have become the strongest. There are so many things they aren't getting from each other, so many things to make them angry, that they may even come to hate each other.

But even then, some of the loving feelings remain. Even when the people fight most of the time and seem to hate each other, loving feelings come once in a while. People may not be able to admit this to others, and even to themselves, but loving feelings are still there. They just aren't strong enough to make the parents want to stay together.

DO PARENTS WHO STOP LOVING EACH OTHER STOP LOVING THEIR CHILDREN TOO?

The love of parents for children is most often stronger and lasts longer than the love of parents for each other. Most parents continue to love their children throughout their whole lives. Even when their children are grown up and have children of their own, they still love their children and think of them often.

Although parents may wish to divorce each other, parents do not divorce children. In fact, a parent cannot divorce a child. Even when there is a divorce, and the parents are living apart, both parents usually continue to love the children. Even though they may hate each other, they both usually still love the children. I like to think of this as three people in a triangle, shown in this picture. The picture shows how a girl can love and be loved by *both* her mother *and* father, even though the parents hate each other.

It is important to remember also that there is nothing wrong with your loving *both* parents, even though they may dislike and even hate each other. If both of your parents love you, there is nothing wrong with your loving both of them. Each parent may not want you to love the other and may try to make you feel guilty about such love. But if the other parent is loving toward you, you should feel free to love in return, and there is no reason to feel guilty or bad about your love.

It is sad to say that it sometimes happens that a parent doesn't love his or her own children. Fortunately, this doesn't happen very often. But even when there is a parent who divorces and leaves the children as well, the children still have the other parent. A man has only one wife and a wife has only one husband. When a divorce takes place, there is no extra husband or wife right there in the house to replace the person who has left. When one parent leaves a family with children, there is another person still there in the house to take care of the children. And if the parent who leaves doesn't love the children enough to want to take care of or visit them, then there is usually still another parent who is there to love and take care of them.

ARE CHILDREN WHO LIVE WITH TWO PARENTS ALWAYS HAPPIER THAN CHILDREN WHO LIVE WITH ONE?

Some children who live with only one parent are jealous of *all* children who live with two parents. They think that all of them are happier. If you live with one parent and believe this, you are giving yourself extra sadness that is unnecessary. Many children living with two parents are worse off than you.

More important than the *number* of parents you live with is the *kind* of parent or parents you have. Bad parents, whether one or two, cause children to be unhappy, and good parents, whether one or two, help children grow up healthier and happier.

2

LETTING OUT THE FEELINGS YOU HAVE ABOUT THE DIVORCE

There are some parents who believe that letting out feelings is wrong. They think that fine, upstanding people stay calm no matter what happens.

I think that these parents have the wrong idea about feelings. I believe that feelings can be very useful. People who hold back their feelings will not make use of them in helping solve problems.

FEELINGS OF SADNESS

Letting out sad feelings helps you feel less sad about what has happened. When I was a boy there was a song that teenagers liked to sing. It was called "If Your Sweetheart Sends a Letter of Good-Bye." The first two lines of this song were:

If your sweetheart sends a letter of good-bye,
It's no secret you'll feel better if you cry.

I think that this advice is very wise. After you cry, you feel better, especially in your head and chest. People who don't cry may continue to feel miserable, and they keep having a full feeling in their head and chest.

Divorce is something to feel sad about, and you should let out your sad feelings, not bottle them up. So if a parent says to you, "Big boys and girls don't cry,"

tell that parent what I have said here. Even if your parent doesn't agree with me, or can't change because he or she has been that way too long, this doesn't mean that you shouldn't cry if you'd like to.

But there is something important I'd like to add here. The important thing is this: it's good to let out *some* feelings, but not *all* feelings at any time and any place. Crying a lot at first is fine and will help you feel better. But if you go around sad and miserable all the time and stop doing things like schoolwork, playing with friends, and chores around the house, then there is too much sadness. And that's going to make you feel worse, not better.

FEELINGS OF ANGER

Most children get very angry when parents separate. This is normal, because there's a lot to be angry about.

A parent is leaving the house, and home will never be the same again.

Anger can be useful. When the anger is let out in small amounts, it can help you. It can help you get what you want. It can help you get rid of feelings that are bothering you. And anger helps you fight harder for the things you want.

If you hold your anger in, and don't let it out, then you won't be using it to help you. You won't be using it to help you get the things you want. You won't be using it to help you get rid of the feelings that are bothering you. And you won't be using it to help you fight. When you let out anger, in small amounts, it helps you fight harder and better.

Take this example of twin brothers. One was afraid to let out his anger. When other children teased and picked on him, he wouldn't fight back. And so he got teased and picked on even more.

14

But when someone picked on the other twin, he did fight back. He would sometimes even fight a boy who was a little bigger than he. Because of this, hardly anyone ever picked on him.

I have said that it is good to let anger out in *small amounts*. It is not good to let it out in big amounts. Then you can get into a lot of trouble. A person who lets out anger by screaming and cursing and biting and hitting a lot of people is letting out too much anger. That person is not going to have friends, and people are going to be very angry at him or her.

It is also a good idea to let anger out when you *first* begin to feel it. If you hold it in, then it grows and grows, and then it may come out like a volcano bursting. When you let it out at the beginning, it is small enough for you to use it to help you. When it gets built up inside and then bursts like a bomb, it's not going to work well for you. Then it just goes all over the place, not just exactly where you want it to go.

FEELINGS OF GUILT

Another kind of feeling that children often have after parents separate is *guilt*. Guilt is the feeling most people have when they think they have done something wrong. But sometimes the person *hasn't* done anything wrong at all and still feels guilty. This kind of guilt is not useful to have. This is the kind of guilt I am going to talk about here.

There are some children who have been brought up to believe that it is a terrible thing to be angry at a parent. And if bad words come into their minds about their parents, they think this is even worse. In my opinion, it is normal, at times, to have angry feelings toward a parent. It is normal for children to have dirty words come into their minds at times—dirty words about their parents. Of course, it's not a good idea to use such words to your parents. Generally, it's a better idea to use more polite words when letting out anger toward parents. With your friends, however, when adults aren't around, I think it's all right to use such words at times.

There are some children who feel very guilty about such ideas. They have the wrong idea. And if their parents have taught them this, then their parents, in my opinion, have the wrong idea. Such parents don't know that angry feelings are normal for everyone, including the anger of children toward their parents. I have never in my whole life met a child who doesn't have such thoughts and feelings toward a parent. I hope that if you have had such guilty feelings about your anger toward your parents, that reading this has helped you feel less guilty.

Another kind of guilt some children feel is guilt about the divorce. They think that it was their fault that their parents decided to separate. They may think that it was because they were bad.

For example, a girl who thought her parents' separation was her fault might beg her father not to leave the house. Over and over she might say such things as "Please, Daddy, don't leave. I know you're leaving

because I wasn't good. I know you're leaving because I hit my brother, and I wouldn't go to sleep when you told me to, and I watched too much TV. I promise I'll never, never be bad again. I promise I'll never ever hit my brother again. I promise I'll always go to sleep when you tell me to. I promise I'll never watch TV again. I promise I'll always be good—forever and ever. Daddy, please, please don't leave!" Even though her father told her over and over that he was not leaving because of her, she still kept thinking it was her fault. Even though he told her that the separation had nothing at all to do with her watching TV too much, she still kept thinking that she had caused her father to leave the house.

This girl's main problem here was that she wasn't thinking clearly about the things that a child *can* control and the things a child *cannot* control. By believing that she had the power to bring about the divorce, she could believe that she had the power to stop the divorce as well.

If you believe your parents' divorce was caused by your being *bad* and that you can stop it by being *good*, you have to learn that there are things in life that a child can control and things that a child cannot control. For example, a child cannot control the movements of the sun, moon, and stars. A child cannot control thunder and lightning. A child cannot control which programs come on TV. And a child cannot control whether or not parents get divorced. There are many things, however, that a child can control. A child can control whether or not he or she does homework. A child can control hitting a brother or sister. A child can control how much TV he or she watches. And a child has the power to do things with substitutes, so that he or she will feel less sad about the separation.

When you see that there are many things that you can control and many things that you cannot control, you may feel better about this problem. And when you accept the fact that you cannot control your parents' divorce—but can control doing things with substitutes for the parent who has left the house—you will feel even less guilty. And after you actually do things with these other people and have fun with them, you will feel less sad about the separation. And then you will not be bothered as much by thoughts that the divorce was your fault. Later in this section I will tell you how to find substitutes.

FEELINGS OF SHAME OVER THE SEPARATION

Some children feel ashamed that their parents' marriage has broken up. They may try to hide it from their friends. They may tell no one about what has happened, even their best friends. They may even lie and talk as if their father were still living in the home when he no longer is. They may stop inviting children into their homes, because they fear that others will see that both parents are no longer living there. And when friends come to the house and notice that the father never seems to be there, they may make up excuses like saying that he is often away on business trips or that he works late on weekdays and even works on weekends.

If you are doing this you are causing yourself extra problems. First, you should realize that there is nothing to be ashamed about when parents get a divorce. It is a sad thing to have happened, but nothing for you to be ashamed about. But even when one, or both, of the parents may have done something to be ashamed of, you have not done anything yourself for which you should be ashamed.

Another thing that you may be doing is giving yourself a new fear that you don't have to have. If you make the divorce a big secret, then you have to go around scared that others might find out. And when other children do find out what has happened, they lose respect for you. They don't trust what you say as much, because of the lies. And they may like you less, because no one likes a liar.

MAKING BELIEVE THAT THERE IS NO PROBLEM

Some children make believe that there is no problem when their parents separate. They deny that their parents are getting a divorce, even though they are living in separate places and even though their lawyers are writing all the papers necessary to get the divorce. Making believe that divorce doesn't worry you helps you feel a little better for a while. However, denying what's happening is really going to make you feel worse as time goes on. By looking at the problem and thinking about it, you may be able to do something about it. Making believe that it isn't there will result in your doing nothing, and the problem is likely to grow and get worse.

THE IMPORTANCE OF TALKING ABOUT WHAT'S BOTHERING YOU

Probably the most important advice I can give you is: *Speak up and say what's on your mind*. Tell people what's bothering you when it *starts* to bother you. Tell about it when it has just begun to bother you. At that time, you will probably not be *very* upset. Then you will be able to solve many of the problems *early*.

I am not saying that speaking up will always solve the problem or get you what you want. I am only saying that that's the best time to try. If you keep things inside, if you bottle up your thoughts and feelings, you will not be doing anything to solve your problems. Many of the problems I talk about in this book come when children do not speak up early enough.

3

SPECIAL PROBLEMS YOU MAY HAVE IF YOU LIVE WITH A DIVORCED PARENT

In this chapter, and the chapter that follows, I am going to talk about the kinds of problems that children may have when living with a separated or divorced parent. Because most children in such a situation live with their mothers, I will often use the word *mother* when talking about the parent with whom the child lives. I do this because it makes writing about it easier. However, if you are living alone with your father, then

just substitute the word *father* when I use the word *mother*. Because most of the problems are the same in the two situations, children living with just a mother or a father should find what I say here useful.

Children living with a separated or a divorced parent have many different kinds of feelings and problems. Some of these cause them extra trouble and worries. In this chapter, I will talk about some of these feelings, especially those that cause problems. And with each problem feeling, I will tell you what you can do to help solve the problem.

BEING AFRAID THAT YOU MAY BE LEFT ALL ALONE

After one parent has left the home, some children fear that the other parent may leave as well. They may think "If my father can leave the house so easily, why can't my mother leave also?" They may then fear that they will be all alone. They may imagine that there will be no one to take care of them, to feed them, to buy them clothes, and to do all the other things that parents do for children.

If you feel this way, it is important for you to appreciate that you still have two parents. If one can't or won't take care of you, the other usually can. I often compare the situation to the parts of the body. You have two eyes, two ears, two arms, and two legs. If something happens to one of these parts of the body, you still have the other side to take over and do most of the things that have to be done.

You may also be afraid that if your father was asked to leave the house, you may be asked to leave as well. You may think such things as "If she told my father to get out of the house, why can't she throw me out also?"

You will feel better if you understand that it hardly ever happens that a parent throws children out of the house. Of course, it sometimes happens that a parent will get very angry at a child and say such things as "I'm sorry I ever had children" or "What a relief it would be if I could get rid of those kids." Usually, such parents don't *really* wish that they never had children or would *really* want to get rid of them. They say these things when they are angry or upset. When they feel better, they are sorry they said such things.

One thing that you can do that can make you less afraid of being left alone is to spend time alone together with whichever parent you are with, at least once each day.

The plan works this way. On the days when you are with your mother, ask her to set aside some time when the two of you can be alone together. During that time, do something with her that you *both* enjoy. You may like reading stories during this time, or playing games.

Sometimes you may want to walk and talk, or listen to music and sing. The important thing is that you do something you both enjoy. And even though your mother may be very busy, ask her to do the same thing with each of the other children as well. And ask your father to do the same thing with you when you are with him.

If you and your parents will get into the habit of doing this *every day*, and make such times alone together more important than anything else, then your fears of being left alone are likely to go away. In fact, doing this each day can make many other problem feelings disappear as well.

BEING AFRAID TO SHOW ANGER AT EITHER PARENT

Children whose parents are divorced may fear letting out any anger they feel toward their father who has left the house. They may fear that they may see even less of him if they were to tell him when they are angry. Some children may also be afraid to let out any anger they may feel toward their mother with whom they live. They may fear that if they were to do so, she might also leave the house.

Children who feel this way may become very timid and shy. They may become very tense. Some get knots in their stomach or headaches. Sometimes they blink their eyes a lot and have other kinds of nervous problems that come from being afraid to let out anger. So if you have such problems you would do well to tell your parents what is bothering you.

LETTING OUT ANGER AT THE WRONG PARENT

Some children who are afraid to tell their fathers that they are angry at them will let out on their mothers the anger they feel toward their fathers. Father then

becomes "Mr. Good Guy," and he can do no wrong. For example, when a boy is with his father, he is a model child, and everybody praises him and says how good he is. This same boy, however, may make his mother the "bad guy." He may be a big brat in his own house. He may refuse to do anything his mother asks. He may swear at her, throw things at her, and cause her a lot of trouble.

If you do this you would do well to remember what I said before: that no one is perfect, that everyone has both good and bad parts. You would do well to take your chances and tell your father the things that are bothering you. When you become less angry at your father, there will be less anger to let out on your mother. You will then have less trouble with your mother, and you will probably have a better relationship with your father also.

COPYING PARENTS WHO FIGHT

There are children who see a lot of fighting between their parents even after the divorce. They may be very angry about this and *copy their parents in the way they let out their anger. They then start cursing a lot, and throwing things, and become very mean to others.*

Children who copy their parents in this way may behave very badly not only at home, but in school as well. They may become very disorderly, make a lot of noise, call the teacher bad names, pick on other children, and make a big nuisance of themselves. They may also bully other children in their neighborhood, and lose all their friends.

Such behavior can cause you extra problems, problems that are not necessary. So instead of letting out your anger after it builds up, as your parents do, you would do much better to express your anger early, before it builds up. The best way to do this is to talk to the people with whom you are really angry. Although it is hard for children not to copy their parents, you should try not to copy them when they are not behaving themselves properly. Otherwise, you will get into a lot of trouble.

BEING BAD TO GET EXTRA ATTENTION

When divorced parents fight a lot, the children may get to feel very lonely. The parents are thinking so much about their fighting that they have little time to think about the children. The children may find that when they are good, their parents continue to ignore them. But when they are bad, the parents interrupt their fighting and pay attention to them. Even though they may get punished, and even though the punishment may be painful, they think that it's better to be punished than to be ignored and lonely.

These children don't realize that they have a third choice. It's not just a choice between being lonely and being punished. So if this is your problem, speak up and tell your parents how lonely you feel. By telling your parents that they are forgetting all about you because they are fighting so much, you can often get the loving attention you want. But you may not get as much of it as you might want if you don't speak up and ask for it.

PLAYING ONE PARENT AGAINST THE OTHER

There are some children who use their parents' fighting to get things for themselves. A girl, for example, may learn that her father is nicer to her and will bring her presents when she sides with him against her mother. Her father is most kind when she agrees with him when he speaks badly of her mother. And he is likely to be unkind when she doesn't agree with him when he criticizes her mother.

The same girl, when she's with her mother, may agree with her that the father is a terrible person. In this way, she may get many favors from her mother that she might not have gotten. This is called *playing one parent against the other.*

Some children will play their parents against each other in a different way. They will complain about one parent to the other. They know that the parent to whom they are complaining is likely to believe them, no matter how big the lie. They know that each parent is so angry at the other that each one will believe practically any bad thing about the other person. This is called *using a parent as a weapon.* It is almost as if one parent were being used like a club or stick against the other.

A boy, for example, who is angry at his mother may tell his father about many unkind things his mother has done to him. Actually, the mother may not have been so unkind. In fact, she may not have been unkind at all. The boy knows, however, that if he complains about his mother to his father, his father will immediately get angry at his mother and do unkind things to her. In this way, he gets his father to help him do the mean things he wants to his mother.

If you play one parent against the other, you are not only going to increase the amount of fighting that your parents do, but you're not going to feel good about yourself either. No one likes a liar. And although you may get a few extra presents or loving feelings or an outlet for your anger in the beginning, you will end up losing respect for yourself and the respect and trust of your parents. I hope you can see what a big mistake this is.

BEING USED AS A WEAPON BY YOUR PARENTS

Just as there are children who use parents as weapons, there are parents who use children as weapons in their battles. When parents are living apart and are still very angry at one another, they may not be able to hurt one another directly. Because their children travel back and forth between the parents, they can be very useful in saying and doing the angry things that the parents can't.

A mother, for example, may keep telling her children how rotten their father is. Hour after hour, day after day, and week after week, she may continue to tell them what a terrible person their father is. If she does this enough, they may come to fear him and even hate him. Things may get so bad that they may even refuse to see him. And when he tries to visit, they may even hide from him or lock the door in order to prevent him

from coming into the house, or shout curse words at him through the windows or even throw things at him.

It is very sad when a thing like this happens. Although there are some fathers who really want to harm their children, they are very, very rare. Most fathers love their children very much.

When one parent criticizes the other once in a while—and does it in a calm voice—it may be that the criticism is true and the children may find it useful to know. If, however, a parent is criticizing the other parent most of the time and if it is done with a lot of rage and screaming, it is likely that everything that is being said is not completely true.

Try to find out for yourself what is good and what is bad about each parent. Use your own eyes and ears and rely on your own experiences. If you believe everything bad that one of your parents says about the other, and then start saying the same angry things, without checking first, you may lose out on getting a lot of love and affection from your other parent.

BEING USED AS A SPY OR A TATTLETALE

Because children travel back and forth between divorced parents, they have a lot of information that each parent might like to have about the other.

A father, for example, might like to know how the mother is spending money. He may be interested in knowing whether she is spending it on the children or whether she is using it mainly to buy things for herself or even for other people. He also might be interested in knowing whether the mother is going out with new men.

A mother might be very interested in knowing whether the father is spending lots of money—money that he might be giving to her and the children. She also might be interested in knowing whether he has met new women he likes very much.

You should realize that you may be helping your parents in their fighting if you carry tales back and forth. And you will usually feel bad about yourself. You would do better to refuse to answer questions about your other parent that you suspect would cause trouble. That way, you won't become a spy or a tattletale.

4

THE EXTRA RESPONSIBILITIES CHILDREN HAVE AFTER SEPARATION AND DIVORCE

When two parents live together, each one has the other to help take care of the house and the children. But as soon as a mother and father separate, each one has extra work. Children then *have* to help out. And I think this is good because it helps them grow up.

Here I will talk about the various things that children can and should do to help parents when they are separated. I will talk not only about how these things can be helpful to your parents, but about how they can be useful to you as well.

HOW YOU CAN HELP YOUR PARENTS

The older children are, the more help they can be to parents. But even younger children can do many important things. If you are old enough to read this book, you are old enough to do many useful things for each of your parents.

Now what are these things? You can make beds, dust off the furniture, take out the garbage, rake leaves, straighten up your room, help with the shopping, fold the laundry, and all sorts of things. Older children can learn to cook and to use a sewing machine, and both boys and girls can learn to use tools to fix things around the house. Older children can also help take care of younger children.

It sometimes helps to make lists. This makes everyone sure that the different kinds of jobs are equally shared. In this way, everyone can be certain that no one person gets too many of the harder or dirtier jobs, while another person gets too many of the easier jobs. Putting a check mark on the list after a job has been done lets everyone know that it's been completed. It can also give you a good feeling when you put down the check mark.

In some families, a certain time of the week is set aside to do the big jobs. Then everyone pitches in together and works. This can often give everyone a good feeling as they work together.

Sometimes it is a good idea to have weekly meetings to discuss problems over the cleaning that may have come up during the week. At the meeting, people can make complaints about things that have happened that they don't think are fair. At that time, they can decide what to do with a person who doesn't do his or her job. For example, the person who cooks may decide not to prepare food for the person who doesn't clean up. Or there will be no TV watching until the garbage is taken out.

Now, I know that *all* these things do not sound like fun. But who ever said that everything in life should be fun? Of course it's important to have fun. But it's also important to learn that there are times when one has to do things that aren't fun. People who only want to have fun and nothing else are not likely to get very far in life. And having to do jobs around the house can help you get used to doing things, at times, that aren't fun.

HOW HELPING A PARENT CAN BE USEFUL TO YOU

Although *all* jobs and chores may not be fun, they can at times be *very enjoyable*. Cooking is a good example. Making a meal that everyone enjoys eating can make you feel very good about yourself. Changing a messy room into one that is spic and span can make you feel proud about what you have done. Learning to do different jobs around the house, like cooking and sewing and repairing things, makes you feel more grown up.

Doing good deeds for other people can give a person a very good feeling. In fact, I think it's one of the greatest and most enjoyable feelings a person can have. When the whole family pitches in together and works as a team, it makes everyone feel good. It makes people feel closer together, and this is part of love.

5

GETTING SUBSTITUTES FOR THE PARENT WHO HAS LEFT THE HOUSE

When your teacher is absent, the person who teaches you that day is called a *replacement* or a *substitute*. You can also find substitutes for a parent who has left the house. If you do, you will feel less lonely about your parents' separation and divorce.

I am not talking here about substitutes who come to live in the home. I am talking about people you can be with outside the home. Younger children must rely on their parents to help them get substitutes. Older children can get replacements on their own.

Earlier, I spoke about a song that many people, especially teenagers, used to sing when I was younger. The name of the song was "If Your Sweetheart Sends a Letter of Good-bye." As you may remember, the song said that if your sweetheart sends a letter of good-bye it's no secret you'll feel better if you cry. If I had written that song I would have written it this way.

If your sweetheart sends a letter of good-bye,
It's no secret you'll feel better if you cry.
  Then, when your chest is clear
  Find another who is dear.
Then you'll no longer ache, pain, and sigh,
For that sweetheart whose letter said good-bye.

Getting a substitute helps you get rid of the sad and painful feelings that people have when they cannot be with someone they love.

WHO ARE GOOD SUBSTITUTES?

Who are the people who can be good substitutes? First, there are the people in your own family. Brothers and sisters, especially those who are older, can sometimes do the things that parents do with children. Doing more things with uncles and aunts can sometimes be helpful too. A grandfather can often be a good substitute for a father, and a grandmother a good substitute for a mother.

Although friends in your neighborhood and school cannot be like parents, they can help you feel less lonely. Having fun with them can help you forget about your sadness over your parents' separation.

It is also good to have a close friend with whom you can talk about the things that are bothering you. Such talks can help you feel better about what has happened with your parents.

There are some children who come home from school and spend most of their time alone thinking about their troubles or watching lots of TV. This is a bad idea. It is far better to go out, play, visit people, and do things. Then you won't feel so bad about your problems.

SPECIAL CLUBS FOR CHILDREN OF DIVORCE

There are also many clubs for parents and children who live in homes with only one parent.

Probably the biggest and most famous of these clubs is *Parents Without Partners*. It has chapters in most cities in the United States and Canada. These clubs have many activities that give you a chance to meet substitutes.

For children living without fathers, there are other fathers with their children. These are sometimes called *Substitute Fathers Groups*. And for children living without mothers, there are mothers with their children. These are called *Substitute Mothers Groups*.

These groups do many fun things together. They go on picnics, camping trips, and visits to museums. They have beach parties. They go to sporting events and also take children bowling, ice skating, roller skating, and swimming. Sometimes groups get together to do things like cooking, sewing, or just shopping in stores. And they often have big dinner parties called "potluck suppers" where every family brings some food and all share what has been brought.

Not only do you have a chance to meet substitute parents at such clubs, but you can meet other children there as well. This is especially useful if you have few, if any, friends in your school or neighborhood. As I have said before, spending time with friends will help you feel less sad about your parents' divorce.

For older children, there are discussion groups and "rap sessions" where young people can talk about the special problems children of divorce often have. Talking with others in your situation can often help you solve some of your problems. Getting advice from other boys and girls whose parents are divorced can be very useful,

because they know exactly the kinds of troubles you have.

Other clubs that can be useful are *Big Brothers of America* and *Big Sisters of America*. In the Big Brother and Sister clubs things are more *personal* than in *Parents Without Partners*. In these clubs, a special man visits with a boy, and the two of them usually do many things together. They may become very good friends. Or a special woman may spend a lot of time with a girl, and the two may become very close. Such people make very good substitutes for the absent parent.

In closing this chapter, I would like to remind you of a very important thing. The world is a very big place. There are billions of people in it. There are substitutes for anyone who has gone away. But they usually just don't come knocking at your door. You and the parent with whom you live have to make efforts to find such people. Sometimes it's easy, and sometimes it's hard. But it's always possible.

6

SPECIAL EVENTS THAT PARENTS ATTEND

There are many events in a child's life that two parents usually attend.

At school, there are open-school days when parents are invited to sit in their children's classrooms and watch what is going on. And both parents are usually invited to teachers' conferences where they are told about how their child is doing.

School plays are often very important too. During the performance, most children think about their parents sitting in the audience and watching. They are usually hoping that they will do well and that their parents will be proud of them. And when one or both parents do not come, children are usually very sad and disappointed.

Besides school events, there are other special occasions that are very meaningful. Certain religious services like confirmations and Bas or Bar Mitzvahs are usually very important. And when one parent isn't there, some of the fun is taken away, and the proud feelings are less strong.

Most children want both of their parents to attend special sporting events like Little League championship games, or the final play-offs in tournaments. They also hope parents will come to scout troop events such as potluck suppers and advancement ceremonies. And on visiting days at camp, a child often feels very lonely when only one parent comes.

WHY SOME PARENTS DON'T COME TO SPECIAL EVENTS

The main reason why parents do not come together to such special activities is that they just don't like being with one another. They may even get very upset just seeing each other. And they may be so concerned about this that they may not consider your feelings.

HOW TO PERSUADE YOUR PARENTS TO COME

Tell them exactly how you feel when only one of them comes to a special event. Ask each of them why he or she doesn't wish to come when the other is there. Most often, the reasons given will not be good ones.

Try to get your parents to understand that they are making *their* problems become *your* problems by not coming to the event. Try to get them to see that just because they are angry at each other is not a good reason for not attending one of these special occasions. You might even want to show them the things I have said here and tell them how important I think it is that they both attend special events. You may get them to change their minds and come.

WHAT TO DO IF THEY STILL DON'T COME

If after you have told them how you feel, they still won't both come, then there is little you can do. But it is important to remember that having only one parent come to a special occasion does not mean that there is anything wrong with you. There are many other children whose parents are divorced, and both of their parents too may not wish to come to these special events. It also doesn't mean that you are not *as good* as those children who have two parents attending. It only means that your situation is a little *different*. Being different is not the same as not being as good or worthy.

SPECIAL PROBLEMS OF WORKING PARENTS

Sometimes both parents do want to come, but one or even both cannot attend because he or she must work. After a separation, there is less money to go around. And a parent can't come to every event because he or she can't afford to risk losing a job over missing too much work. However, most working parents will arrange to take time off, and will even be willing to lose some money, for a *very* important event.

If you have a working parent who *never* comes to your special events, you have to realize that the problem is in the parent, not in you. Such a parent probably has less love for you than you would like. This does not mean that such a parent has *no* love for you at all. It means that there is *less* love than you would like. I have spoken before about mixed feelings and about how there are different amounts of love that a parent can have for a child. I have also spoken about how there is something wrong with a parent who does not have very much love for his or her own child.

Remember that there are others who can love you more. You have to get love from these other people, whom I have called substitutes. And some of these substitutes may even come to your special events.

7

VISITING WITH YOUR OTHER PARENT

Because it is more often the father who leaves the home, I will speak here about children who are living with their mothers and visiting with their fathers. However, if you are living with your father and visiting with your mother, then substitute the word *mother* whenever I say *father*.

Now, you may find this a hard thing to believe and think there must be something wrong with me if I can say such a thing, but some children actually get to spend more time with their fathers after a separation than before. When living at home, many fathers spend lots of time with work or watching television. Many fathers work part of the weekend. Others may be home on weekends, but may spend little time with their children anyway. When a separation takes place, many fathers may spend more time with their children because they want to make up for the time lost when they can't be with them at all. Fathers usually love their children very much, and they feel terrible about the fact that they will no longer be living with them.

YOUR FATHER'S NEW PLACE

If your father has not yet decided exactly where he is going to live, ask him to try to find a place where there will be a special place for you and your brothers or sisters, if you have any. Some fathers have enough money to get one or more rooms for the children to stay in when they visit. Other fathers do not have enough money for this. Even if your father can't afford a separate room, at least ask him to set aside a special place for you and the other children. It's best for each child to have his or her own special spot, if this is possible.

It's also important to get your father's new telephone number as soon as he has it. You may want to put the number in a special place or hang it up on a bulletin board. This helps to remind you that you can get in touch with your father whenever you want. Of course, he will not always be home. But it's still good to feel that you can call him when you want to.

Also ask your father if it's all right to call him at his office or place of business once in a while. I say *once in a while* because it's not a good idea to call him often where he works. This can interfere with his job.

It's also a good idea to ask your father to take you to see the place where he'll be living as soon as he's definitely decided where it will be. It will make you feel better to know exactly where your father is going. It's especially helpful to see the place before your father actually leaves the house, and it's also a good idea to visit your father's new place as soon as possible after he leaves. Then you become even more familiar with it, and it makes you feel closer to him.

REASONS WHY FATHERS VISIT WITH THEIR CHILDREN

Most often, separated fathers visit with their children because they love them very much and want to be with them often. They want to have some kind of family life even though they are no longer married. Unfortunately, sometimes other reasons get mixed in as well—reasons which have little, if anything, to do with love.

Sometimes a father will want to spend time with the children because of *guilt*. Although he usually wants to see the children because he loves them, the guilt reason is there also. He feels bad that the family has broken up.

A little bit of such guilt, in my opinion, is fine. It can cause the father to spend more time with the children and do more things with them. If, however, the guilt is the main reason for seeing the children, then the father is not going to enjoy himself very much after a while. The children too will then enjoy the visits less.

If you think that this is happening with your father, talk to him about it. It may be a good idea for you and your father to see each other less. Then both of you are likely to enjoy the shorter visits more.

Sometimes one of the reasons fathers visit a lot is that they want to prove that they can be better parents than the mothers are. This is called *competing*. Such fathers may want to see their children not only because they love them, but also because they want to use the children to compete with the children's mother. One way of telling if your father is doing this is to see if he asks you a lot of questions which compare him with your mother. Another way to tell is to see if he boasts about all the things he does for you and, at the same time, tells you how little your mother does for you. If he is comparing himself to your mother a lot, this is probably one of the reasons he is visiting.

If your father is doing this, tell him that you do not want to get involved with it. Tell him you don't want to answer his questions about your mother. Tell him you don't want to be a spy or tattletale. Tell him that he is taking the fun out of the visits by comparing so much. Tell him also that he should be doing things because *he* wants to do them, not because he thinks they are better or worse than anything your mother does with you. You may find it hard to tell your father things like this but if you can get up the courage to say the things I have said, you may get him to stop.

Some fathers visit not so much because of feelings of love but because of a sense of *duty*. They think that it is important for fathers to visit their children even if they don't want to very much. A little bit of this reason is fine, in my opinion. It's when duty becomes the main reason for the visit that trouble starts. Then fathers may be spending more time with their children than they would like, and so both come to be bored or to dislike the visits.

If you think your father is doing this, talk to him about it. Tell him that his visiting you from a sense of duty does not help make the visits enjoyable. If he stops spending extra time with you from a sense of duty, you'll all be better off, even though you'll be spending less time with him.

WHEN FATHERS MAKE YOU ANGRY ·

Sometimes children are angry at visiting fathers because they come late. If this is happening to you, the best thing you can do is to tell your father how angry it makes when he is late. Tell him you don't like hanging around wondering when he will come. Ask him how he feels when he has to wait for someone and he doesn't know when the person is going to show up.

If, however, after talking to him he still shows up late, then it's best to accept the fact that this is one of your father's bad habits. In that case, it's best to try to

do something else while waiting in order to take your mind away from thinking about when he's going to arrive. It's best to play games with other children, or read a book, or do some homework, or watch TV while waiting for him. Then the waiting becomes easier, and you won't be so angry about the lateness.

Children are also often angry at fathers who break promises. All fathers may do this once in a while, and it's important to remember that this is normal. For example, a father promises to take his children to the zoo. When the day comes, there's a big rainstorm, and so they can't go. Instead, they go to the movies. Breaking such a promise doesn't mean that the father is bad or doesn't love the children.

But these aren't the kinds of fathers I am talking about here. Here I am talking about fathers who break promises very often and the reasons are not very good ones. They may promise to take a child somewhere and then give some silly excuse for not doing so. Or they may say that they forgot.

If this is happening to you, it's important to tell your father how this makes you feel. It's best to do this while you are calm, before the anger has built up and is exploding. Perhaps talking to him will get him to try harder to keep his promises. If it doesn't, then it's best not to keep trying to get something that you can't. Accept the fact that this is one of his bad habits. Don't expect him to keep his promises, and then you won't be so disappointed. Enjoy the things about him that you can. Stop trying to change the things that you can't.

FEELING GUILTY ABOUT VISITS

Some children feel very guilty when they go off with their fathers and leave their mothers alone, especially on holidays.

A little bit of such guilt is normal and healthy, in my opinion. It shows that the child is sensitive and cares about the mother's feelings. On many holidays, a mother is likely to be very lonely when she cannot spend it with her children. There can be a problem here, however, if the child comes to feel too guilty and feels so bad about leaving a mother at home that he or she does not enjoy visiting the father.

Often, children who feel so much guilt are being made to feel guilty by their mothers. Their mothers may be telling them how lonely and sad they feel when they are left alone. Such mothers may be saying things like this in the hope that the children will change their minds and not want to go with their fathers. Or they may want to get extra attention or pity by saying such things.

If your mother makes you feel very guilty about

leaving her, it is important for you to try to find out if she is doing the kinds of things I have just talked about.

If she is trying to get you to feel so guilty about leaving her that you will change your mind about seeing your father, tell her that this is not fair. Tell her that you want to see your father and he wants to see you, and that it is important that you do so.

If she is trying to get attention or pity by saying such things, tell her that this is no way to get someone to be interested in her. Tell her that that kind of talk makes you want to spend *less* time with her, not *more*. These may sound like harsh things for a child to say to a mother, but they can be useful things for such a mother to know. In addition, they can get her to stop saying things to make you feel guilty.

Sometimes it is the father who tries to make the children feel guilty about the fact that he is alone. And he may do this for the same reasons that some mothers do. So if your father is saying things that make you feel guilty about spending certain times with your mother, talk to him about it. Try to find out his reasons and then tell him the things I have just told you. In this way, you'll be doing something to solve this problem.

Some children feel guilty if they kiss their father in front of their mother when their father comes to pick them up. Some even feel guilty if they have a happy smile when their father first arrives. At times, a mother may say that it makes her sad to see how glad the child is to see the father.

It is my opinion that if you want to kiss your father when he comes to visit you, and if your father wants to kiss you, then you should do it. If your mother tells you not to, tell her about the things I have said here. Perhaps she will stop. If, however, it still makes her feel bad, then it might be best for her not to be in the same

room when your father arrives. But she should be the one to leave the room. It's her problem that she can't stand to see you enjoy seeing your father. She shouldn't ask you to meet in another place.

Sometimes it's the father who doesn't want the child to kiss the mother in front of him. If your father says this, tell him what I have said here, and try to get him to see that what he's asking is not fair.

If parents start to fight when the father comes to pick up the children and when he brings them home, children sometimes feel that the fighting is their fault. They may think that if the father didn't come to pick them up, then there wouldn't be all this fighting. This is a wrong idea. The visits just give such parents an extra chance to fight. Such fighting is not the child's fault.

One way to avoid giving parents a chance to fight

in this way is to ask your father to meet you outside the house. All your father has to do when he arrives is to honk the horn of his car or to ring the bell. Then you can meet him without his having to get together with your mother. Or a meeting between parents can be avoided if your father picks you up at school at the end of the school day. Then you might return to school from your father's house early in the morning of the next school day.

THINGS YOU CAN DO TO MAKE VISITS MORE ENJOYABLE

One important thing that can make a visit more enjoyable is to be sure that both you and your father are doing things you *both* like. If your father does something that you like and he doesn't, then he's bound to get bored or fussy after a while. In the same way, if you do something that your father likes and you don't, you're likely to get tired and fussy very soon. It is important that both people plan together what they want to do. It's important also to speak up and say how you feel.

Sometimes a visit can be more enjoyable if you are allowed to bring along a friend. Most adults find it hard to spend long periods of time doing things that children enjoy. If you spend part of the visit playing with friends, it makes it easier for both you and your father. It's also a very good idea to make friends in the neighborhood where your father lives. Many children have two sets of friends: one group where their father lives and one group where their mother lives. This can make the visits with their fathers much more fun.

It is also important that you and each child in your family has the chance to spend some time alone with your father when you visit him. During this time, the

two of you might want to walk, or talk, play some game, build something, listen to music together, or do some other thing. It's not so important what the two of you do. What is important is that you do something that you both enjoy. This can make both of you feel closer to each other, and this is one of the most important things in life.

Often, the piece of paper that the court gives parents when they get divorced tells exactly how much time each parent should spend with the children. Sometimes the amount of time is too long for the children, and other times the children feel they aren't getting enough time with their fathers on the visits. If this is happening to you, speak to both of your parents and see if you can't get things changed.

THINGS THAT CAN HELP MAKE A VISIT MORE USEFUL

Not all the time alone together has to be fun time. Some of it should be spent doing serious and important things. One useful thing that you and your father can do is to talk about problems you may be having. If there are things that your father is doing or saying that you don't like, this can be a good time to discuss them. Or if you have any other kind of worries, or troubles, or problems on your mind, this is a good time to talk about them. In this way, you may "get things off your chest" and then feel better.

One thing that can make your visits useful is to help your father take care of his house. Helping him with cleaning, shopping, fixing his car, and doing other chores around the house can be very useful. It not only helps him, but it helps you. It makes him feel proud of you, and it makes you feel proud of yourself.

WHAT IF YOUR FATHER DOESN'T VISIT WITH YOU

There are some fathers who hardly ever visit their children. They come around once or twice a year, sometimes without even telling anyone in advance that they are coming. There are even fathers who see their children less than that, and may only send a birthday card or a Christmas card once in a while. Everyone will agree that these are not very good fathers. They have very little love for their children, or no love at all.

If your father hardly ever visits you, this does not mean that there is something wrong with you. The problem is not that you are unlovable. The problem is that your father cannot love. The problem is in him, not in you.

The first thing that you should do is to tell your

father how angry you are that he has shown so little interest in you, so little love. Sometimes saying this can get such a father to become more interested and spend more time with you. But usually fathers who are this unloving are not likely to change and start showing more interest.

In such cases, it's best to give up trying to get something that is impossible to obtain. It's better for you to spend more time with substitutes and get love from them. When you stop wishing for your father to love you more, you will become less angry.

8

MONEY, MONEY, MONEY!

In most families, fathers earn more money than mothers. Because of this, when there's a divorce, the father usually has to give money to the mother so that she can pay the rent and buy food, clothing, and the other things children need. Sometimes a mother earns no money at all, and so she must rely entirely on the father.

The most common complaint by divorced mothers is that the fathers are not giving them enough money. And the most common complaint by divorced fathers is that the mothers are asking for too much money. And each usually complains that the other is spending the money on the wrong things. Fighting over money can last for days, and weeks, and months, and even years! If your divorced parents fight over money, you may not be able to tell who is right. And you probably can't do anything to stop your parents from fighting. Still, it is important for you to understand certain things about money.

MONEY IS NOT THE MOST IMPORTANT THING IN THE WORLD

The first thing you must learn is that money isn't the most important thing in life. After hearing all that talk about money over many months, and even years, you may get the idea that there's nothing more important in the world than money. This is a wrong idea.

I am not saying that money is not important at all. It is very important. I am just saying that there are certain things that are more important—things like health, having friends, loving people, being loved, giving to others, honesty, and being sympathetic to other people's problems. It is the kind of person you are that determines how happy you will be, not the amount of money you have.

Everybody has heard about rich children who are lonely and miserable, and poor children who are very happy. Having money makes it easier to be happier. But it's not the most important thing. The kind of person you are is much more important.

LEARNING TO DO WITH LESS

When parents divorce, the same amount of money may have to pay for two rents, two electric bills, two gas bills, and two water bills. There may be extra travel expenses for the children to go back and forth between the parents. An extra car might have to be bought.

Because of these extra expenses, you may have to give up things that you enjoyed before. You may go on fewer vacations. You may have to stop going to summer

camp. You may not be able to eat in restaurants as often and may have less expensive and tasty foods to eat at home. You may not have as many clothes as before. Even the toys you get for birthday presents may be less expensive.

Although these changes may make you feel sad and even angry, it is important to remember what I said before. Money—and the things that money can buy—are not the most important things in life. It's the other things I have mentioned, things like the kind of person you are and how you treat other people, that will determine how happy you are going to be.

WHEN A FATHER STOPS SENDING MONEY

It sometimes happens that a father stops sending money entirely or sends very little money. The mother then usually gets very, very upset and angry. One thing that some mothers do when this happens is to stop letting the father see the children. Sometimes the mother's lawyer will get a judge to agree with her that this is a good idea. The judge then will tell the father that if he doesn't send the money he can't see the children.

I think that this is a bad idea. I think that such a mother should try to get her money in other ways. I think that it is *very* important that children continue to see their father after a separation. Even if a father is being cruel to a mother, this should not be a reason for preventing him from seeing his children. Such a mother is hurting her own children for something that is not their fault.

So if your father is not sending the money he should, and if your mother is not letting you see him, tell her what I have said here.

However, your mother is not the only person you should talk to about this. You should talk to your father as well. You should tell your father that what he is doing causes you to love and respect him less. Although he still has good parts that make you like him, this is one of the very bad things that causes you to lose respect for him. Tell him that you have to go without things you would like to have because he is not sending your mother money, and that this makes you angry at him.

If you tell him these things, perhaps he will change his mind and start sending your mother money again. If he doesn't, tell him that if he starts doing other things that hurt you and your mother, then you might reach the point where you yourself might not want to see him. Then you and your mother will be in agreement, and then it would be a good idea that your mother and the judge stop him from visiting with you.

I know that these are hard things for a boy or girl to say to a parent. But if you can get up the courage to speak up and say these things, you might be able to change the situation. Telling your mother what I have said might get you to continue seeing your father. And telling your father the things I have said might get him to start sending money again. Such talking is a good example of the importance of *speaking up*.

WHEN A MOTHER WORKS

Before the separation, a mother may have been home most of the time, or she may have worked part of the time. After the divorce, she may have to work much more if the family is to have enough money.

When children are young, a working parent has someone at home to take care of them. This person can be a housekeeper or a grandparent or other relative.

If you are taken care of by someone else when your mother is at work, it is important that you like that person. I hope that you do, and that that person likes you very much too.

If, however, you do not get along well with that person, it's important to talk with your mother about it. Sometimes it is the person's fault. When that is so, then the mother should try to solve the problem or find another person.

But perhaps it's your fault. You may be very angry about the fact that your mother isn't always there. And so you don't like any substitute at all, no matter how nice and loving that person may be. If that is the way you feel, then you are just causing yourself extra problems. If you would just stop hoping for the impossible—that your mother will quit work—and let yourself enjoy being with this other person, you will be much better off.

9

WHEN PARENTS GO OUT ON DATES

WHY DATING IS IMPORTANT FOR PARENTS

Although parents usually love their children and like being with them most of the time, they enjoy spending time with adults as well. Most grown women like to spend some time with men. And most grown men like to spend some time with women. Your mother, then, no matter how much she loves you, is going to want to spend time with men. And your father, even though he may love you very much, is going to want to spend some time with women. When a man and a woman go out together, that is called *dating*. The woman is called the man's *date*. And the man is called the woman's *date*.

Just as you like to have fun, so do your parents. On a date, people enjoy each other's company. They eat in restaurants, see movies and plays, go to concerts, and do many other things together that they enjoy. Most parents work very hard and need to have fun sometimes, too.

CHILDREN WHO GET UPSET WHEN A PARENT HAS DATES

A child who doesn't want a parent to go out on dates is being selfish. The child is not thinking about the parent's feelings—the things *he* or *she* needs and the things that can make *him* or *her* feel good.

There are some children who even try to stop a mother from dating by getting sick just before she is ready to go out. They may get stomachaches, or headaches, or start vomiting. Usually, children who do this are not really sick. They make believe they are sick so that their mothers will stay home. If such a mother does stay home, she will usually be very angry at the child who does this. In addition, the mother's new friend may get angry at the child as well. And this is sad because this person might have turned out to be a good friend for the child also.

If you are angry at a parent for dating think about what I have just said. Remember that parents are entitled to fun. Then you may be less angry if they go out once in a while.

BEING MEAN TO THE PERSON A PARENT DATES

Many children get very angry at a parent's date. They blame the date for taking their mother away from them.

Some children try to get rid of a mother's date by saying things that are going to make the man feel uncomfortable. They may be old enough to know that it will embarrass both the mother and her new date if a child says to the man, "Are you going to be my new daddy?" Other children are purposely bad when a date comes to the house. They also want to scare the man away so he won't want to marry their mother.

If you are being mean to your mother's new friend, you may be doing a foolish thing. The man may be a person with whom you could also have a good time. He would be a very good parent substitute. I spoke before about how important substitutes can be, and a mother's new friend can be a very good one. Also, when a mother is out on a date, you don't have to sit around

angry and lonely. You can still have a good time with a baby-sitter. Or if you are older and no longer need a baby-sitter, you can play with a brother or sister or spend time with friends. Having a good time with such substitutes can help you feel less lonely while your mother is out on a date.

SHOULD CHILDREN MEET ALL THEIR PARENTS' DATES?

There are mothers who do not have their children meet each new date. There are others who have every new date meet them at the house and who introduce each one to their children. They say that this is the honest thing to do.

But many children get very upset when they meet one date after another. Some keep hoping that each new man will marry their mother and become their father.

If that is how you feel, I believe you are better off

not meeting each new person. A mother who meets her dates somewhere else is not being dishonest; she is, in my opinion, being considerate of her children's feelings.

So if your mother is dating many men, bringing each one to the house, and this makes you upset, tell her that it bothers you. Tell her also exactly what upsets you about what she is doing. Perhaps she will listen to your complaint and meet her dates somewhere else. But when she meets someone whom she likes and sees often, then I believe she should bring that man to the house even if you tell her you don't want her to. He may turn out to be a good friend and a good substitute.

Most fathers do not have their children meet every new date. They usually see new women friends at times when the children are not there. For this reason, you aren't likely to have the same kinds of problems about meeting all his new friends.

WHEN PARENTS TAKE YOU ALONG ON A DATE

After a parent meets a man or a woman whom he or she sees very often, the parent may bring the children along when they go out together. And when the children join their parent and the parent's new friend, they can have lots of good times together. However, one of the problems that children sometimes have is that the grown-ups may want to talk to each other more than they want to talk to the children. The children then feel ignored and angry.

If this has happened to you, I think it would be a good idea to speak up and tell your parent and your parent's friend how angry it makes you to be ignored. Often, if you complain in a nice way, they will pay more attention to you. They will then share their time with you. Sometimes they will talk with each other and sometimes with you. You can't ask them to pay attention to you all the time. But you should ask them to pay attention to you some of the time if they aren't. This is just another example of the importance of speaking up—something I have talked about many times before in this book.

If, instead of talking about the problem, you start fighting, making a mess, and having temper tantrums, you will only get your mother or father angry. You may even get punished for what you are doing. And this only makes things worse. Now you are not only getting less attention, but you are getting punished as well. Had you spoken calmly to your parent and let out your anger early, you would have gotten no punishment and probably would have gotten more attention.

It is also important for you to realize that a parent's date can be a new person with whom you can do many enjoyable things. No one person can be interesting and fun all the time. With another person there, it is more likely that different things will happen. And if you and your parent's new friend start liking each other very much, this can make everyone happier. Having a third person who can like and even love you can help make up for the loneliness you have felt since the separation. And having a third person to love can make you feel better about yourself. Loving feelings make two people happier—the person who is loved and the person who loves.

WHEN A DATE BRINGS HIS OR HER CHILDREN

Sometimes a parent's date will have his or her own children. After your parent has gotten to know this person well, the children may be asked to come along and meet you.

There are things about this situation that you may like, and there are things you may not like. I will talk about each separately.

First, what are the things about this that can be good? The new children can be fun to play with. This is especially true if you and the date's children are about the same age. And when the date brings along his or her own children, then you may be less bothered when the adults spend a lot of time talking together. You will then have the other children to play with while the adults are spending time together. If your parent is thinking about living with or marrying the date, then it is good for all the children to get to know one another very well.

There are many things, however, about the date's children that might cause you to be unhappy. You may not like them and they might not like you. Sometimes you have good reasons not to like one another, and sometimes you don't. Sometimes there is nothing wrong that anyone is doing, it's just that you are different kinds of people. Sometimes your ages are so far apart that you just don't enjoy playing together. But sometimes there are troublemakers who make the experience a sad and difficult one for everybody. I hope that those who are reading this book are not the ones who are the troublemakers.

If there is a lot of trouble with the other children, it's a good idea to discuss the problem with your parent, the date, and the other children. Often, the problem can be solved, but sometimes it cannot. Then the children just have to learn to put up with one another, or the parents may decide not to bring the children together as often. But it's far better to try to solve the problem, because then you and the other children can have a lot of fun together. When you can't solve it, you may both lose out on a lot of good times with one another.

Learning to *share* with the other children is important if you are going to get along well. And when you give something, you usually get something in return. But even if it doesn't even out, giving can make you feel good about yourself. Helping the date's children have a good time can make you feel good about the fun you have given others.

10

WHEN A PARENT'S FRIEND
SLEEPS OVER

As you may know, when a man and woman like each other very much, they usually enjoy kissing and hugging each other. They may even like to sleep together in the same bed all night.

Here I am going to talk about some of the problems children may have when a parent's friend sleeps over. Because most children live with their mothers, I will talk about the times when a mother's man friend sleeps over. But the same kinds of problems can come up when a father's woman friend sleeps over. So if you want to find out what to do if your father's woman friend sleeps over, just substitute *father* for *mother,* and *father's woman friend* where I say *mother's man friend*.

Some children do not mind when a mother's man friend sleeps over. They have gradually gotten to know and like the man. They think then that it's only natural that he stay over at the house.

If the man, for example, wants to spend both Saturday and Sunday with their mother, they think it would be silly for him to go home late Saturday night and then come back again early Sunday morning. It doesn't bother them that he sleeps over in their mother's room. They may even like it more than if he were to go home and come back, because if he stays over they can play with him early in the morning. They might even

look forward to coming into their mother's bedroom in the morning, jumping around on the bed, wrestling and playing fun games.

There are some children, however, who may like the mother's man friend, but don't like him to sleep over. They themselves like to cuddle with their mother but don't like the idea of anyone else doing so. They are jealous of the man and wish they could sleep in their mother's bed just like the man is doing. Their mothers may have even said that they are too old to be sleeping in a mother's bed, and that only very young children do this once in a while. And yet, this man, who is much older than they are, is allowed to. They may think this isn't fair.

What can you do if you feel this way? As I have said many times in this book, it is always a good idea to talk to the person who is doing something that bothers you. Sometimes the talking helps, and sometimes it doesn't. But it's almost always a good idea to try.

However, this is one of those situations where talking is probably not going to get your mother to change. It probably won't get her to stop having the man sleep over. She has probably been very lonely since the separation and wants very much to love and be loved. She often wants and needs the new man friend very much, and sleeping with him makes her feel very good.

When you do talk to your mother about this, she might explain these things to you. She might give you her reasons why it is important for her that the man friend stay over. Perhaps then, when you understand better her reasons, you will be less angry at her.

Another thing that can help you feel less angry about a mother's man friend sleeping over is learning to share more. If you are to get along well with other people, it is important to share. If a friend comes over to play with you and you don't share your toys with him or her, that child is not likely to come back. If you want a friend to play with you and no one else, that child may get angry. In the same way, you can't have your mother all to yourself. You have to share her with others, whether you like it or not. When a man sleeps over with your mother, it doesn't mean that he has all of your mother and you have none of her. You can still spend time with her, love her, and cuddle with her at times. If you learn to share in this way, you will feel less angry about a man's spending time with your mother and sleeping over at the house.

The kinds of mothers I have just spoken about are those who only have a man friend sleep over when he is someone special in their lives. There are some mothers, however, who do not believe that it is important that they know a man well before asking him to sleep with them in their homes. They do not believe that they should do this with only one person who is special. They may do this with many men.

Most children are bothered when a lot of men sleep over. They are angry because it seems like everyone in the whole world can hug, cuddle, and sleep with their mother except them. It seems like they are sharing their mother with a long parade of people.

I think that these children have a right to be angry. I think that mothers who do this are not being fair to their children. I believe that such mothers are causing their children to feel too many jealous feelings.

If your mother is doing this, it is very important that you tell her exactly how you feel about it. Try to get her to change her mind about what she is doing. Telling her the reasons why you don't like what's happening is the best way to get her to stop inviting all these men to sleep over. You might even want to show her what I say here about why it's a bad idea for her to do this. Perhaps she will then stop; perhaps she won't. If she doesn't, then you can at least say that you tried.

If she doesn't stop, there is little you can do about this now. You can spend more time doing things you like and being with your own friends. This will help you feel less sad and angry. And it is also important to remember that the older you get, the more time you'll be able to spend away from home. In this way, you will not have to see many of these men. And finally, you'll be old enough to leave home. Then you won't have to be involved at all.

11

WISHING PARENTS WOULD
GET TOGETHER AGAIN

There are children who keep wishing their parents would get together again. They may keep wishing this for many months and even years after the parents have separated. They may continue wishing for their parents to marry again even after they have gotten divorced. And they may even wish this to happen after one or both parents has gotten married to someone else. They keep hoping that their parents will divorce the new people and get married to each other again. Although their parents may have told them *many times* that they are *never* going to be married to each other again, they keep wishing for it to happen.

It's normal to wish this once in a while; it's not healthy to keep thinking about it much of the time—especially if months and even years have passed since the separation.

MAKING PARENTS FEEL GUILTY TO GET THEM BACK TOGETHER

Some children keep telling their parents how sad and miserable they have been since the separation. They try to make their parents feel sorry for them. They may say such things as "Look how sad and miserable you've made me" or "How can you do such a terrible thing to *me*?" They hope that their parents will

70

feel so guilty over the separation that they will get together again.

Other children may get sick with stomachaches, headaches, and other illnesses in order to make parents feel guilty. Sometimes they realize what they are doing, and sometimes they don't. But whether they realize it or not, the sickness is not real, it is faked to make the parents feel guilty about the separation.

Sometimes children even run away from home in order to get their parents back together again. They may leave a note before they run away which says something like this: "I've run away from home because of the separation. Now you'll see how bad you made me feel. Now see what you've made me do. I'll come home if you promise never to separate again in your whole life." By doing this, they hope to make their parents feel so lonely that they will be willing to get back together again if only the child will come home.

If you are trying to make your parents feel guilty so they will get together again, try to realize that this hardly ever works. And even if it did, your parents' problems would not be solved. So they would still be unhappy with each other, and you would still be living in a home with much fighting and sadness.

Running away in order to make your parents feel guilty can even cause new problems for you instead of solving the problems you already have. When you return, you may be surprised that your parents aren't as happy as you expected them to be. You may even be amazed that you are punished.

Remember that when a child runs away, parents are usually very, very upset. They miss the child very much. They are very frightened for the child and may fear that the worst things may have happened to him or her. Also, they are very angry at the child for doing this

to them, for causing them so much worry. So when the child returns, the parents have mixed feelings. They are both happy and angry at the same time. They are glad that the boy or girl has returned and so want to hug and kiss the child very much. But they are usually so angry, as well, that they want to punish the child with the worst possible punishment. And it may take a long time for them to forgive the child for all the worry and grief he or she has caused them to suffer.

WHAT YOU CAN DO TO STOP WISHING YOUR PARENTS WILL GET TOGETHER AGAIN

If you keep wishing that your parents would get back together, even though they have been separated and divorced for many months and even years, you may not have learned the difference between things you can control and things you cannot control. You would do well to read again the things I said earlier about control and thinking that the divorce was the child's fault.

When you learn to accept the fact that you cannot control certain things—and get substitutes so that you feel better—you may stop wishing that your parents would marry each other again.

Wishing that your parents will get together again can also be helped if you remember that it hardly ever happens that divorced people get married to each other again. This is especially true when one or both of the parents has married someone else.

12

WISHING PARENTS WOULD GET MARRIED AGAIN

Most children gradually get used to the fact that one of their parents will not live in the house and that he or she will not change his mind and return. After they get used to this idea, many children start wishing that the parent with whom they live will get married again. Or they may wish that the parent that they visit will marry again. They may even think about moving into the house of the parent they visit if that parent gets married again and the one with whom they live does not. What they want most of all is a whole family with a mother and a father and children—all living together.

SHOULD A PARENT MARRY AGAIN TO MAKE YOU HAPPY?

There is only one good reason for a divorced parent to get married again. And that reason is that the parent wants to for his or her own sake. It's a very bad idea for a parent to get married again for the children's sake. People should marry only if they like and love each other very much. Otherwise, they are bound to be miserable with each other.

If your mother is divorced you don't need just any old daddy around the house. You need a daddy who loves your mother and gets along well with you. It's not a situation where any daddy will do. And the same is true for a father and a new wife. The new wife can't be just anyone if you are going to be happy. She has to be someone whom your father loves and whom you get along with. If not, everyone is going to be *very* unhappy.

But sometimes parents do get married anyway because of the children. The parent thinks that it will be all right that the new husband or wife isn't loved very much. The parent thinks that just having that person around the house will be good for the children. But what happens in such situations is that the adults get to be more and more unhappy because they don't love each other very much, if at all. They then start fighting, and the whole problem starts all over again. The children then suffer.

I hope you can see now why this is such a bad idea for a parent. I hope you can see also why this is such a bad idea for the children.

SHOULD YOU HELP DECIDE WHETHER A PARENT MARRIES AGAIN?

A parent's decision whether or not to get married again should be based on whether the parent likes and loves the new person, not whether the child does. If the child doesn't like the new person, he or she should try to get along better with that person.

Your parent might, however, ask you about your

feelings toward the new person. Then you might be able to give your parent some useful information that might help him or her decide whether to marry or not. Children's opinions can be useful here in *helping* the parent make the decision. But the children's opinions should not be the final and most important factor in the parent's decision.

For example, one boy said to his mother that her man friend was nice to him when she was around but that he wasn't so nice when she was not there. The mother then watched her friend closely and began to see that he was a phony in many ways. So then she decided not to marry him. But it wasn't because the boy said, don't marry him. It was because he had given her important information that was useful to her in helping her make her decision.

In a different situation, a girl told her father that his woman friend was mean to her and that she ignored her. But when the father watched the girl, he discovered that she was very jealous and wanted her father all to herself. No matter how much attention the woman friend gave her, it was not enough. So the father decided to marry her anyway and eventually the girl got used to sharing her father with someone else. Then they got to like one another much more and the girl was glad her father had not listened to her.

THINKING THAT A PARENT'S REMARRYING WILL SOLVE ALL YOUR PROBLEMS

Some children believe that all their loneliness will end if a parent marries again and they can once again live in a home with two parents and children.

I agree that such a home is the best kind, *if* it is a happy one. But even in the best and most happy homes, there are problems. If you think all problems will be solved if your parent remarries, you are making a big mistake. You are going to be very disappointed when you find out that this isn't true. Every home has its problems. And the home in which parents have married again is no exception. The new home may solve some of the problems. But it won't solve all of them. It may add new ones as well. So remember this if you keep dreaming that your life will be perfect and continually happy if only your parent would get married again. It won't be perfect. It will be a mixture of good and bad.

13

SOME IMPORTANT THINGS TO REMEMBER

Separation of parents is a big change in a child's life. Change causes new things to happen. And new things are always scary at first. I say *at first* because as time goes on most people get used to new things, and then they aren't as frightening.

What I have just said is so important that I am going to repeat it. As time goes on, we get used to new and strange things, and they become less scary. And that is exactly what happens to most children whose parents separate. At first, they are very, very afraid of their new way of life. They are especially afraid of the part that has to do with living with only one parent. After a time, however, they get used to the new way of life and become much calmer about everything.

Besides living with only one parent in the home, boys and girls have to get used to other things as well. For example, their parents usually change.

A mother may have to go back to school in order to learn something that will help her earn money. The extra work may make your mother tired and she may get angry and fussy more easily. Your father, too, may have to take on more work in order to pay for the extra expenses caused by the divorce. This may make him tired and grumpy at times.

Both parents, however, may be much happier after the separation. After many years of fighting, the separation may be a big relief. Now, for the first time in years, they may also be enjoying themselves.

For this reason, both parents may begin to pay much more attention to their appearance. Your mother may spend more time putting on makeup and nail polish and fixing her hair. She does this so that she will be more attractive to other people. Making herself prettier is going to help her make new friends and perhaps among them find a new husband. This, of course, can help you get a substitute for your father. Your father may also want to date and possibly marry again. So he may start being more careful about the clothing he wears because he wants to make himself more attractive too.

As a child of divorced parents you may have to get used to the new ways your parents are behaving. It may almost seem that you have new parents. I hope that the changes that take place for your parents after the separation are good ones and that they then become happier people to be with.

Another problem that children of divorce sometimes have is that they keep imagining that things were *great* before the separation. They seem to forget all the fighting and remember only the good things that happened before the separation. And they may only think about the bad things that happened after the separation and not the good things.

This kind of thinking can add to your troubles. It can even make you feel miserable. If you have been thinking this way you would do well to remember that both before and after the separation both good and bad things were happening. It wasn't great before the divorce and it's not likely to be great after. Both times have good and bad parts. That's how life is for all people, whether or not their parents are separated. The important thing is to enjoy the things that you can in the present and not waste time thinking about the past. You can't change the past, but you can do things that can make the future better. The things I tell you about in this book have little to do with the past. They are about the present and the future, and how you can make them better if you're willing to try.

Part II

LIVING WITH A MOTHER
WHO HAS NEVER BEEN
MARRIED

MOTHERS WHO AREN'T MARRIED

Most children who live with one parent have another parent who was once married to the parent with whom they live. The other parent has either left the home or died. But there are some one-parent families in which the parent, usually the mother, has never been married. Here I will talk about such families.

WHY SOME WOMEN DON'T MARRY

Women who would like to be married but who stay single instead usually do so because they haven't met the right person. And they would rather not marry at all than marry a person they didn't like very much.

There are also women who don't ever want to get married. They like to be completely independent, and so they prefer not to have a husband.

HOW WOMEN WITHOUT HUSBANDS HAVE CHILDREN

Many women who don't marry feel very sad about the idea of going through their whole lives without having any children at all. They love children very much. More than anything else in the whole world, they want to have one or more children of their own.

How then do such women get babies? They usually do this in one of two ways. Some find a man that they like and have sexual intercourse with him. This means that the man puts his penis into her vagina, just like a husband and wife would when they want to have children. Sperm comes out of the man's penis and connects with a little egg inside the woman. The egg then starts to grow into a baby. This is called *getting pregnant*. This is the way you started to grow. And this is the way every person in the whole world started to grow as well. That's one way to get a baby started. The other way is to go to a doctor who puts some sperm into the woman's vagina. The doctor gets the sperm from a man who sells or gives his sperm to the doctor for women who want to have babies this way.

Some women are not married and get pregnant by mistake. They have sexual intercourse with a man and do not take care to stop the sperms from meeting with the egg. They then have a choice. Some go to a doctor who takes the growing egg out of the woman's body. This is called an *abortion*. Others decide to let the baby grow. When the baby is born, the woman has another choice. She can give the baby to someone else who will bring it up. This is called *adoption*. Or she can keep it herself. Often, the mothers who do this are very loving. They are so loving that they do not want to have an abortion. They are so loving that they do not want to give the baby up for adoption.

WHY SINGLE WOMEN WHO BRING UP THEIR CHILDREN ARE USUALLY BRAVE AND CARING

They are brave because they know they will probably have to do all the work of bringing up the child themselves. And they are brave because many people do not respect them because they have children without having husbands.

Unfortunately, there have been people, both in the past and in the present, who think that women who do such things are less worthy than others. They do not respect such mothers and may laugh at them or call them bad names. Some consider such women bad and sinful. I personally do not.

I believe that there is something wrong with a person who thinks less of a woman who decides to have a child when she doesn't have a husband. Such a mother is usually a very loving person and does not deserve to be disliked or looked down upon by others for having a baby. Wanting to grow a baby inside oneself and then raising a child is one of the most beautiful things in the world.

DON'T BE ASHAMED IF YOUR MOTHER ISN'T MARRIED

Children whose parents are not married are sometimes called *bastards*. These days, the word bastard is a dirty word. But there was a time, hundreds of years ago, when it wasn't. A person who was a bastard was simply one whose mother and father were not married. There was nothing considered wrong in being a bastard, and few looked down upon them. Today, however, it has come to be used as an insult.

If your mother is not married and someone calls you a bastard, I think it's important to realize that there is something wrong with the person who calls you this. Such a person is hateful. There is something wrong with that person's thinking if he or she can believe that your parents' not being married is a reason to call you bad names. There is nothing wrong with *you*. You have

nothing to be ashamed of. You have done nothing wrong. It makes you no better or worse than anyone else.

Most people will judge you by the kind of person you are. If you are nice and friendly and kind to others, you will be liked, and you will have friends. If you are not nice and friendly, then you probably will not have too many friends. These are the things that really count, not whether your mother and father were married.

Some of the greatest men who ever lived had mothers and fathers who were not married. Some lived at times when they were not laughed at or looked down upon. Others grew up at times when such people were. Fortunately, we are living at a time when people whose parents are not married are not being looked down upon as much as they used to be. And this, as I am sure you will agree, is a good thing. People are becoming smarter about this and are becoming less cruel.

2

THE FATHERS OF CHILDREN WHOSE MOTHERS AREN'T MARRIED

WHERE ARE THE FATHERS?

Most children whose mothers are not married do not grow up knowing their fathers. There are many good reasons for this.

Sometimes the mother does not know who the father was. Or she may have decided not to have any further contact with the man who is the child's father. Sometimes the mother may want to see the child's father again but he went away, perhaps without even knowing that the mother became pregnant. And, if a doctor put the father's sperm in the mother, the man who gave the sperm may not want the mother to know who he is.

WHY IT IS DIFFICULT TO MEET YOUR FATHER

If your mother knows who your father is *and* she also knows how to get in touch with him, then she *and* the father have to decide whether it would be a good idea for you to see him. In every family situation of this kind, there are *three* people involved, *all* of whom should agree that it would be a good idea for the child to see the father.

The first person, the child, usually has no trouble making the decision. Most boys and girls want to see their father very much.

The second person, the mother, *may* think that it's a good idea, but most often she thinks it's a bad idea. She may know that the father will not be interested or might be unpleasant and cause a lot of trouble.

And the third person, the father, also has to want to meet the child. But he may have a family that doesn't know about the child, and he doesn't want to tell them. He may feel that he wants to forget everything about the child he had earlier, or he may be afraid that if he sees that child he'd start to love it, and then he'd be involved with two families.

In my opinion, it's not just enough that you want to see your father; your father should want to see you as well. Otherwise, he may feel forced into seeing a person he doesn't want to see. When this happens, the father is going to be angry. And he's not going to have the kinds of loving feelings toward you that you want.

Another reason why it is often difficult to meet your father if your mother isn't married is that your mother may not know where he lives. So if you want to see your father, first ask your mother if she knows where he is or if she knows how to find out.

What can you do if your mother really doesn't know where the man is, and has no way of finding out? The answer is *nothing*. There is no way that you can meet your father and you would do best to accept this fact.

I agree that it's better to know who one's father is and to be able to meet him. But it's not the worst thing in the world if one doesn't. One of the worst things any child in such a situation can do is to go around thinking all the time about who his or her father is. Even more foolish is to go around looking for the father and asking people if they know where he is. Thinking this way and searching this way is just a waste of time.

If you are in such a situation you would do far better to go about your own life and do the things other children do, like learning, playing, working, and spending time with friends. You would also be wise to find the kinds of substitutes that I have spoken about in other parts of this book.

If your mother *does* know where your father is, but doesn't want you to see him, she should say just that. She should not lie to you and pretend she doesn't know how to find him. That is a bad idea.

What can you do if your mother says *yes* she knows where your father is, but *no* she doesn't want you to see him? Ask her to give you the reasons why and then have a long talk about this. Once you understand the reasons you may change your mind and agree that it's not a good idea for you to see your father.

On the other hand, after listening to you, your mother may change her mind and agree that her reasons were not good ones. Then she has to find out if your father wants to see you. If he doesn't, then I do not think it's a good idea for you to keep trying to see him—he won't be much of a father to you anyway. It is true that you might feel better just seeing him once or twice because you're very curious and might then be able to stop thinking about him so much. I, however, don't think it's a good idea to force such fathers to see children if they don't want to. So the best thing you can do is to accept this and do the other things I just spoke about. Things like being with friends, learning in school, and being with substitutes.

If, after you and your mother talk, neither has been able to change the other's mind, there is nothing you can do for the time being. You want to see your father and don't believe that your mother's reasons for not allowing it to happen are good ones. Your mother doesn't want you to see your father and has not been convinced by you to change her mind. So you cannot do anything right away. But as you get older, it is a good idea to talk about it again once in a while. Perhaps one of you will change your mind.

IF YOU DO MEET YOUR FATHER

Once in a while, a mother who knows where the father lives decides that it would be a good idea for the child to see him. If the father says yes, also, the child can then meet him.

This doesn't happen very often. When it does, the father and child usually see each other only a few times. Not having lived with each other, the father and child do not feel close, and the child then feels disappointed that a loving relationship did not grow. But at best the child's curiosity has been satisfied, and he or she feels better.

Sometimes, and this rarely happens, the child and

father get to love each other, and then there is a good relationship. But if you are a child in such a situation, it's important not to hope very hard for such a thing to happen, because it hardly ever does.

3

SOME IMPORTANT THINGS TO REMEMBER

There are certain things that I have said in this part of the book that are very important for children whose mothers are not married to remember.

It is important to remember that there is absolutely no reason to be ashamed of your mother if she is not married. Those who do not respect your mother have something wrong with their thinking. And those who would call her names are being nasty and even cruel.

In addition, it is also important to remember that there is no reason to be ashamed of yourself if your mother is not married. You did absolutely nothing wrong. You have not been bad or sinful. Anyone who would call you bad names or respect you less because of the fact that your mother isn't married has something wrong with his or her thinking. Most people will judge you by the kind of person you are. If you are nice and friendly to be with and kind to people, you will have friends. Most people care about the kind of person you are, not whether or not your mother is married.

Remember also that relatives can be very important. Children whose mothers are not married know relatives only on their mother's side of the family and sometimes they are lucky and have many relatives on their mother's side. Other children have very few relatives on their mother's side. They therefore may wish even harder that they knew their father. Then they would not only have a father, but more relatives as well. If you are lonely for more relatives, try to spend more time with the relatives you *do* have. In addition, you have to try to get more friends. Also, if you find the kinds of substitutes I have talked about, you won't feel so lonely.

Everyone in the world loses people who are important to them from time to time. Sometimes important people die and sometimes they go away. But there are always replacements or substitutes. The world is a big place and there are billions of people in it. There are many lonely people who would enjoy having friends. They are there, but they won't often come to you. You have to find them. The older you are the more you can do things on your own to find them. And when you do, you will find that your life can be as enjoyable as anyone else's.

Part III

LIVING WITH ONE PARENT AFTER THE OTHER HAS DIED

1

SOME IMPORTANT THINGS YOU SHOULD KNOW ABOUT DYING

Every living thing in the world must someday die. Many children think that this isn't fair and wonder why this has to be. "Why can't my mother and father and I and everyone else just go on living forever?" they ask. The reason is that if a living thing didn't die—even one kind of living thing—the whole world would soon be filled up with that kind of life.

WHAT IF NOBODY EVER DIED?

Imagine what would happen if only one kind of life, dogs for example, didn't die. Soon the streets would be filled with dogs. Also, dogs would grow older and older and still not die. There would be dogs a hundred years old.

And, after a long time, there would be thousand-year-old dogs.

And, after a very long time, there would even be dogs who were *a million years old*. That, I am sure you will agree, is a very old age for a dog, or anyone else.

By that time, there would be dogs everywhere—millions, and billions, and trillions, and quadrillions of them. There would be mountains and mountains of dogs that would cover everything. And there would be no room for anything else.

Nothing else would be able to stay alive. Also, there would be no room to grow food for all those dogs and so they too would all die. Imagine what would happen if not only dogs lived forever, but all other life forms as well—cats, and rats, and gerbils, and hamsters, and horses, and cows, and pigs, and elephants, and all the other kinds of animals and plants. Everything would get crowded sooner. The whole world would soon become one big crowded mess. And that is why everything must someday die.

Even though death must come someday to everyone, it is still a very sad thing. In fact, of all the sad things I know of, death is the saddest. And of all the different kinds of people who might die, mothers' and fathers' deaths are among the most sad. It is worst of all for the father or mother who has died, because he or she will never again enjoy the pleasures of life. A parent's death is terrible as well for the children who have been left behind, because they will never again enjoy the pleasures of being with that parent.

But if you are a boy or girl whose mother or father has died, it is important to remember that your own life is not over as well, and that there are many things that can be done to help you feel less terrible about what has happened.

WHAT HAPPENS TO A PERSON AFTER DEATH?

For thousands of years, just about everybody who has ever lived has wondered about what happens to people after they die. No one can say that he or she knows for sure exactly what happens. Some people believe that there is a kind of life after death. Even though a person's body is put into the ground, they believe that a soul or spirit still lives. Some believe that there are places called heaven and hell where dead people go. Others believe that there is absolutely no kind of life whatsoever after death. They believe that when someone dies, that is the end of everything for that person—forever. And there are others who, as much as they try, just can't decide what to believe about whether or not there is any kind of life after death. They just say they don't know, one way or the other, and don't spend too much time thinking about it.

At the time a mother or father dies, most children

wonder what is going to happen to the parent. When they ask adults about this they are often confused because some people say the parent still lives in heaven; some say there is no heaven; others say they just don't know; and others say things they don't really believe.

Sometimes an adult will even say to a child, "God loved your Mommy so much that He took her up to heaven to be with Him." I have never met a grown-up who believes such a thing. The person who says this usually does so because he or she thinks that it will help the child feel better. Usually, all it does is to make the child feel angry at God for having taken the parent.

The best thing to do, if this happens to you, is to ask a lot of people to please tell you the honest truth about what they believe happens to people after they die. Getting a lot of honest answers can help you make up your own mind about what has happened.

If an adult gets impatient with you for asking questions like this over and over again, he or she just doesn't realize how important it is for you to speak about your dead parent. Each time you speak about the parent you have lost you feel some pain, but each time the pain gets a little bit less. Repeating thoughts and feelings helps you get used to the death. So if an adult says something like "I've answered that question twenty times, and I'm not going to answer it again. Go away and stop bothering me," tell him or her what I have said here. If the grown-up still doesn't want to answer, then talk to someone else.

If you haven't visited the grave of your dead parent, ask your remaining parent to bring you. Having a picture in your mind that shows exactly where the dead parent is helps answer the question, "Where does a dead person go and what happens to him or her?" It also helps you become less confused about death and makes you feel a little closer to your parent who has died.

2

THOUGHTS AND FEELINGS YOU HAVE ABOUT THE DEATH OF A PARENT

When children learn that a parent has died, they usually have many different kinds of thoughts and very strong feelings. Some of these thoughts and feelings help you feel better. Others can be very upsetting and may add to your troubles. Here I will tell you about some of these different kinds of thoughts and feelings. I will tell you how to use some of the good ones and what you can do to get rid of the ones that might make you feel worse.

CRYING

Sometimes when an adult tells a child that a mother or father has just died, the grown-up says things like "Big boys and girls don't cry," or "See how brave you can be and not shed tears." People who say things like this have somehow gotten the idea that anyone who cries is being childish and weak. I think that these are very foolish ideas.

Crying is part of *mourning*, which sounds just like *morning*. Mourning has a purpose. It helps sad feelings

come out. After people mourn, they feel better about
the sad thing that has happened. If someone feels like
crying and holds back the tears, all the feelings stay
inside and make the person feel even worse. So if
someone says to you that you shouldn't cry, don't listen
to that person. Cry if you feel like it. You'll then see
how much better it'll make you feel.

REPEATING

Another thing that happens when people mourn
is that they repeat the same things over and over.
Thoughts about the dead person keep coming into
their minds. The same thoughts keep repeating themselves. They may keep thinking about the person's dead
body or about different things that the dead person
used to do and say. Sad feelings too keep coming on,
over and over.

Wouldn't it be better just to try to forget the whole
thing as soon as possible? Yes, I agree that it would be

nice if things could happen that way. But most people cannot quickly forget someone they love. So the forgetting takes time. And mourning helps a person forget more quickly. It does this by repeating thoughts and feelings about the dead person. Each time the mourning person thinks about the dead person, he or she feels pain. But each time, the pain is a little bit less than the last time. So the hurt feelings get less and less as time goes on. Of course, when a parent dies, one never forgets completely. There is always a little pain, but mourning helps it get very small.

Some children find that they may want to ask questions about the dead person. They may want to know about what happens to people after they die, whether they ever come back to life, and what happens to the body. Sometimes a grown-up gets angry at a child who asks questions like this over and over again and may say something like "I've answered that question twenty times, and I'm not going to answer it again. Go away and stop bothering me." Such an adult doesn't realize how important it is for a child to keep speaking about the dead parent.

It is a good idea to tell such an adult that it is important for you to keep asking these questions, and if the grown-up still doesn't wish to answer, then talk to someone else. The important thing is to keep asking questions until you have been satisfied.

TREASURES

Another thing that can be helpful in mourning is to get something that belonged to the dead parent that you can keep for yourself. Each time you look at or hold this thing, it reminds you of the dead person and may even cause painful feelings. But each time you do this, the painful feelings get less and less.

Many different things can become treasures. Sometimes a picture of the dead parent is chosen. Sometimes a favorite possession of the parent is chosen, like a father's favorite tie or a mother's favorite bracelet. Sometimes it's a special gift that the dead parent has given the child. Some children keep these things for a short time, others treasure them for many years, even for the rest of their lives.

Sometimes a remaining parent wants to throw out the possessions of the dead parent in order to get rid of the painful feelings as soon as possible. If your parent is doing this, be sure to stop that parent in time to get one or more of the possessions. Tell that parent what I have said here, how useful such a treasure can be.

As time goes on, there is not only less pain over the death, but also good feelings each time the treasure is looked at. It reminds the boy or girl of happy times with the dead parent. And this, of course, is very good.

ACTING LIKE A BABY

Following the death of a parent, some children become babyish. They may start using a bottle again, long after they have given it up. Some may start sucking their thumb, using baby talk, or whining like a baby when they can't get what they want. Such behavior, in my opinion, is common and all right for a short time. So if it makes you feel good to be a little babyish for a short time after your parent's death, I think that's perfectly all right.

However, if you feel like acting that way for a long time, I would suggest you try to act your age. Otherwise, you'll be adding a new problem to the ones you have because your parent has died. Certainly your friends and playmates would consider it a problem and would not want to play very much with you. They might even tease you and laugh at you and call you "baby." Also, you are not likely to feel very proud of yourself if you act in this way.

If in spite of my advice you can't seem to help it, I suggest you talk to your remaining parent about this. He or she may have been going along with your babyish behavior and if you explain that you want to act more grown up, your parent will help you to stop doing this.

BEING ANGRY

We get angry when we can't have something that we want. So when a mother or a father dies, children get angry because they want the parent to be alive again and he or she will never return.

Not only do children get angry that a parent has died, but many children even get angry *at* the parent who has passed away. They may angrily say or think such things as "I hate her for dying" or "He went and died on us and now we don't have any father." Even though they know that the parent didn't want to die, and didn't die to be mean, they still can't help feeling that their misery is the parent's fault, and they are angry at the parent for causing all the sadness and loneliness. They just keep thinking things like "If he didn't die, I wouldn't be so miserable now" or "If she didn't die, my life would be happy now."

It may surprise you when I tell you that such thoughts and feelings are *normal*. Most children have them after a parent dies. Some children, however, feel very bad about themselves for such angry feelings. They think that there is something wrong with them for having angry thoughts toward their parents. They think that other children—better than themselves—would not have such ideas.

This is not true. Other children have the very same kinds of ideas after a parent dies. There is nothing wrong with such angry feelings. So if you think you are terrible because you are angry at a parent who has just died you are adding extra worries for yourself—worries that you do not have to have.

FEELING GUILTY

Here I will talk about guilty feelings that come when a child really hasn't done anything wrong but feels bad about himself or herself anyway. I have already spoken about the kind of guilty feeling that some children have when they think there is something wrong with a person who gets angry at a parent for dying. Here I will talk about other kinds of guilty feelings that children may have after a mother or father dies.

A child may feel very guilty for wanting to play a

short time after learning that a parent has died—even on the same day. And, if an adult says something like, "What kind of a person are you, laughing and running around on the day your father has died?" the boy or girl may feel even worse.

I think that the grown-up who says such a thing is being unkind and doesn't know very much about the way children really are. Such a person doesn't realize that children's feelings change faster than adults' and that play can help children forget the death of a parent and feel less pained about the loss.

Some children believe that a mother or father's death was their fault. They may say, "I know Mommy died because I was very bad. I gave her so much trouble she got sick and worn down—especially because I fought so much with my brother. If she were alive, I'd never fight with him again."

If you feel this way, remember that there are certain things in life that children *cannot* control and others that they *can*. As I have said before, children cannot control the movements of the sun and moon, the waves in the sea, the wind, thunder, and lightning. They also cannot control such things as a parent's getting sick, having an accident, or dying. Children can control what games they play, what friends they play with, and whether or not they do their homework. Think about the difference between the things you can and cannot control.

Sometimes a boy or girl will get so angry at a parent because the parent made him turn off the TV, do homework, or go to sleep, that he or she will think: "I wish she was dead" or "I would be better off if he'd go away and die." Then, if it happens that a parent does die, the child may think that it was his or her fault and feel guilty. But most children don't *really* want their parents to die; the thought just comes when they are very angry and means only that they would want the parent to be away from them for a short time. Such thoughts are normal and most, if not all, children have such ideas once in a while.

If you have had thoughts or wishes that a parent die—and then the parent really does die—think about what I am now telling you. First, thoughts and wishes can't make a thing happen. Second, if you wish a parent dead once in a while, that is a normal wish. And third, a parent cannot die because of a wish; rather, a parent can die only because of sickness or an accident that had nothing to do with your wish.

BEING AFRAID

Another feeling that children often have after a parent dies is fear. Sometimes children are afraid that the other parent will die as well. This hardly ever happens. If you are of the age of most children who read this book, your remaining parent is probably still

young or in the middle of his or her life and has many years to live. Your remaining parent is probably so young that he or she will still be alive when you grow up—when you will be able to take care of yourself. It is *very* rare for both parents to die when they are very young.

One way to find out whether your other parent might die soon is to talk to him or her about your worry. Ask if that parent is sick. Usually, he or she is not and is quite healthy. Look at the parent and see if he or she looks sick. Usually, the parent will look quite well. Ask other people whom you know well and trust. They too can tell you whether the remaining parent is healthy and whether he or she might die. If you do this, you are likely to be less fearful about his or her dying.

Some children become afraid that they will die soon as well. They not only think about the fact that they too will die *someday*, they make the mistake of thinking it will happen soon. But since you are still a boy or girl, there is every reason to believe that you have many years to live and that you will not die until you are very old.

After a parent dies, some children become frightened that if the other parent dies they will have no place to live, nothing to eat and no clothing to wear. If you are afraid of these things, ask your remaining parent what would happen if he or she were to die. It is very important for you to have the answer to these questions if you are to become less frightened about these things.

Many parents even have these things written down in certain papers called a *will* which tells what will happen to their property after they die. A will also tells where you will be staying if both of your parents die. Usually, it is with friends or relatives of your parents. They may be called *guardians*.

If you want to see the will, you should be shown it, in my opinion, even though it may be hard for you to understand exactly what many things in it mean. This can help you feel less scared about what will happen to you if your second parent dies.

There are a few children whose parents have no friends or relatives to take care of them if both of the parents die. Even these children are taken care of. They usually live in places called foster homes, where there are parents and other children. The city pays the mothers and fathers in the foster homes to take care of other children. Although living in a foster home is usually not as good as living with a friend or relatives, it is still a home, and the children there usually get good care, clothing, and food. They go to school from the foster home, and it may become like their real original home.

If your parent has died, and you have been afraid that if your second parent dies also you will have no place to live, I hope that what I have said will make you feel less scared about this.

There is one last thing I would like to say here that is very important. The painful feelings you have after a parent dies get less and less as time goes on. This is a very important thing to remember. It has been said that *time* is a great healer. This means that many kinds of sicknesses and many kinds of painful feelings get better with time. It can help you feel less pained by a parent's death if you will try to remember this.

3

MISTAKEN IDEAS SOME CHILDREN HAVE AFTER A PARENT DIES

MAKING BELIEVE THAT A DEAD PARENT IS STILL ALIVE

Many children do not want to believe that their mother or father has died. They may call the person who tells them a *liar* or may think that the person is joking. I have never met anyone who would be so cruel. If someone whom you know and trust has told you that your parent has died, you should believe it is true. If you make believe that it hasn't happened, you will not be able to do those things that I will tell you about—things that might help you feel less sad about the death.

Some children go back and forth between believing that the mother or father has died and not believing it. They might say, "I know Mommy's dead; but when is she going to make me my supper?" or "When is Daddy going to come home from being dead?" These children don't realize that when you are dead you can never come back—even for a minute. When they get used to this they stop having such confusing ideas.

HIDING THE FACT THAT A PARENT HAS DIED

Other children do a very strange thing. They are ashamed that their parent has died and try to hide it from friends and classmates. They may stop inviting people to their homes because they fear that friends will see that only one parent lives in the house, and their secret will be revealed. Some even make up lies and say that they have two parents but that the dead parent is hardly ever around because he or she goes away a lot on business. Or they may make up a story that the dead parent just never happens to be at home when other boys and girls come to the house. Many of the children who make a big secret of the fact that their parent has died walk around scared that people will learn the truth.

Some of the children who try to hide a parent's death think that it is a terrible thing to be different from others. They believe that anybody who is different is not as good as the rest. I do not think that this is so. If your parent has died you may be different from someone who has two parents, but there is absolutely nothing to be ashamed of about that difference. You have done nothing bad or wrong.

There are some children who hide the fact that their parent has died because they fear that other children might say things like, "He's the one whose mother died" or "She's the girl whose father got killed."

The child whose parent has died may even hear children say such things when they don't know that he or she is listening.

If other children say such things about you, it is important to understand that these children are not making fun of you. In fact, they are usually quite sorry about what has happened. They think and say these things because they are worried and scared that the same thing might happen to them.

Unfortunately, it sometimes happens that children do tease a boy or girl whose parent has died. This is very thoughtless, but you would do well to understand that these children may be scared that the same thing could happen to them, and they cover up their fear by teasing and laughing at you.

If this happens to you, the best thing to say back to the teasers is something like "There must be something wrong with you if you can laugh at somebody who has had such a sad thing happen. There must be something wrong with you if you can be so cruel." Saying that will usually make them stop and make them feel ashamed of themselves.

Trying to keep the death of a parent a big secret just adds an additional and unnecessary problem to the ones you already have. Walking around frightened that others will find out the truth makes you even more unhappy than you already are. Also, when the other children find out the truth, they will think that you may lie about many other things as well. They then may not trust you even when you are really telling the truth. This can make other children less friendly and you even more lonely.

BELIEVING THAT A DEAD PARENT WAS PERFECT

After a parent dies, it is natural to keep remembering only the good things and to forget the bad things. As time goes on, a child may come to believe that the dead parent had no weaknesses or bad parts, only strengths and good parts. The remaining parent, as well, may do the same thing, so the whole family gets the idea that the dead parent was perfect, or almost perfect. A mother, for example, a long time after her husband has died, may say to her children, "There was no one who ever lived who was as loving, and good, and kind, and considerate as your father. They don't make people like that anymore."

If a parent says something like that to you, do not believe it. Tell that parent that no one is perfect and that no one ever was, even your dead parent. Ask that parent to think very hard about the dead parent's faults and weaknesses and tell you about them. Tell that parent that there must have been some, and it is important for you to know what they were. The best picture you can have in your mind of your dead parent is that he or she—like everyone else in the whole world—was a mixture of both good and bad parts. This will help you accept your own weaknesses and be less disappointed about the weaknesses of others as well.

Believing that a dead parent was perfect can make you think you have to be perfect as well. Because this is impossible—no one is perfect—you may then feel bad about yourself for not being perfect, as the parent was supposed to be. Also, believing that a parent was perfect can make it hard for you to get along with other people, both young and old, because none of them is perfect. You may become disappointed with just about everybody, because there are no perfect people.

DOES A DEAD PARENT WATCH OVER HIS OR HER CHILDREN?

There are children who believe that the dead parent can still see everything that happens to them. They may imagine that the dead parent's invisible soul, or spirit, or ghost flies around watching everything that happens to the child. Some children believe that if they do a wrong thing the dead parent will see it, be very angry or sad, and even punish them. Sometimes they may think that the dead parent will get God to punish them for having done a bad or wrong thing.

There are even some adults who believe that this happens. Such a grown-up might say to a child something like, "Your mother in heaven can see everything that you're doing now and it must make her very sad to see what a bad child you have been" or "How can you do this to your poor dead mother who loved you so much?"

But most older children and grown-ups do not

believe such things. They believe, as I do, that such ideas are wrong and silly, that a dead person cannot see what is happening to living people, that there are no such things as ghosts that watch over the living, and that dead people have no way of doing anything to living people either directly or through God.

So if you have such ideas, try to see how silly they are. And if a grown-up tells you such things, ask that person if he or she really and honestly believes what he or she is saying. If the person says yes, then try not to believe it. If he or she says not really, then tell the adult that that was a cruel thing to say because it can be quite scary to believe that a mother's or father's ghost is watching one's every move, and that every bad thing that one does—no matter how small—will be observed and punished.

Sometimes a remaining parent will say, "If your father knew what you have done, he would turn over in his grave." This means that the dead father would get so upset over what the child has done that his body would move about so much that it would turn over in the coffin. This is just another one of those silly ideas that should not be believed. Most often a parent says such a thing to scare a child into being good. Most often the grown-up doesn't believe it. But if he or she is silly enough really to believe such a thing, don't you be foolish enough to believe it as well.

4

LIVING WITH THE REMAINING PARENT

If your father has died, your mother is called a *widow*. If your mother has died, your father is called a *widower*. There are special problems that children have when they live with a parent who is a widow or a widower. I will tell you about some of these problems and what you can do to make it easier for you to live in this kind of family.

UNDERSTANDING HOW A PARENT FEELS AFTER A HUSBAND OR WIFE HAS DIED

When one parent dies, the remaining parent is usually very sad and may cry a lot—for days or even weeks.

Sometimes the parent may not feel like doing the usual things that need to be done, like working or taking care of the house and children. However, because these things have to be done, parents usually push themselves to do them even though they get no pleasure from such work.

Some parents may want to be alone a lot when they feel sad and not want to be with friends, or even the children. Other parents who feel very lonely at such times may try to be with as many people as possible, including the children.

Usually, parents stay sadder longer than children.

However, as time goes on, most remaining parents become less and less sad. They get used to the fact that their husband or wife has died, and they try to get back to living the way they did before. They then become friendlier and more interested in their children and more fun to be with.

So if your remaining mother or father is very, very sad after the death of your other parent, know that as time goes on it is very likely that your parent will become less and less sad. As time passes many painful feelings slowly go away, and sadness over the death of a loved person is one such feeling.

FINDING SUBSTITUTES

One thing that is very important to remember is that there can always be a substitute for your dead father or mother. As I have said, a substitute is a person who takes the place of someone else. Another word for substitute is replacement. When your real teacher is absent, the person who teaches you that day is the teacher's replacement.

There are some children who believe, especially around the time that a parent has died, that there can never be another person who can replace the lost mother or father. This is not so. This is wrong thinking. Although it is true that a real mother or father usually loves a child more than anyone else, there are still others, both young and old, who can love a child almost as much. And sometimes a substitute loves a child as much as a real parent.

There are many different kinds of substitutes. Most children have uncles and aunts, grandmothers and grandfathers, older cousins and other relatives who can be substitutes for a lost parent. Also, friends of your remaining parent can also be good replacements. And your mother or father may one day get married again, and then you'll have a new parent to substitute for the one you lost.

There is no such thing as there being no substitute. You and the parent with whom you live have to think about finding one, and make plans, and work to get one. Sometimes substitutes are easy to find, and sometimes they are not. Sometimes they come to the house on their own. Other times they have to be looked for.

Right after the death of a husband or wife, the widow or widower is usually too sad to think much about finding a replacement. But after some time has passed, most widows and widowers start thinking about and looking for a substitute. If your remaining parent is not doing this, speak to him or her about it. Tell that parent what I have said in this book about how important it is, both for you and for your remaining parent, to find a new person to replace the person who has died.

There are not only clubs for parents where replacements can be found, but there are clubs for children as well. For example, in scouting, Y's, after-school clubs, Big Brother and Big Sister groups, there are adults who can be good substitutes, at least part of the time. Ask your remaining parent to find out about the clubs where you live. Practically every city or town, except the very smallest ones, has one or more clubs of this kind.

IS IT WRONG TO LOVE A SUBSTITUTE FOR A DEAD PARENT?

There are children who find that strong loving feelings have grown for a substitute and think that they are bad for having such feelings. They fear that the dead parent would be very disappointed in them if he or she knew of their love for this new person. They think that if they truly loved their dead parent they would not have such loving feelings for the substitute.

For example, after a mother has died, a father may meet a woman he loves and then marry her. The child may like this new mother very much because she is so warm and kind. After a while, the child may have strong loving feelings toward the new mother but feel very bad about such feelings. He or she may fear that the dead mother will be angry about this love for another mother.

If you think this way you are causing yourself to have extra worries for no good reason. The main thing that any loving parent wants is that the children have a substitute parent as soon as possible if he or she should die. They hope that the replacement parent will be loving and kind to the children and give them the same kind of good care the remaining parent often hopes to

find a new parent that they did. So if you feel guilty, disloyal, and bad about yourself because you love a substitute, you will do well to think about what I have just said. Remember that your dead parent would have wanted it this way and would be happy if he or she could ever know (which can never really happen) that a loving replacement has been found.

WHEN YOUR PARENT HAS DATES

As I explained earlier in this book, *dating* is the word that is used when a man and a woman go out together to have a good time. On dates, people may go to restaurants, movies, shows, or other enjoyable places. They also may spend a long time talking and getting to know one another better. If the two people find that they like one another a lot, they may date quite often. And if two people who date a lot come to love each other, then they may live together or marry.

At the time of the death of a parent, the remaining parent usually feels so sad about the loss—especially if there were deep loving feelings for the dead person— that he or she does not think too much about dating or finding a new husband or wife. However, once a parent has gotten over the early sadness and starts getting back to doing the usual things, thoughts of meeting a new person start coming into the parent's mind. Thinking about finding a substitute is normal. The remaining parent wants to feel less sad and lonely. Meeting a new man or woman to replace the dead parent is one of the best ways to do this. Also, the remaining parent often hopes to find a new parent for the children as well. There-fore, the wish to find a substitute comes from the hope that both the remaining parent *and* the children will then be happier.

But sometimes children think that a parent's dating means that the remaining parent didn't love the dead parent very much. For example, a boy whose father died might say, "If my mother really loved my father, she wouldn't be going out with other men." He may not realize that if his father really loved his wife and children while he was alive, he would have *wanted* his wife to find another man after he died. He would want his wife to feel less sad and lonely by finding a new man. And he would want his children to have a new father.

Many children get angry about a parent's dating. They may want the remaining parent all to themselves and not want to share that parent with other people—especially with dates. If you feel this way you have to learn to *share* the remaining parent with others. You can't have that parent all to yourself. You have to realize that you can't have everything you want. Also, the remaining parent isn't the only one in the world with

whom you can spend time. There are many *other people*, young and old, with whom you can have enjoyable times. Spending time with these substitutes will make you less angry about a parent's dating.

GIVING YOUR REMAINING PARENT EXTRA HELP

When a parent has died, the remaining parent needs all the extra help he or she can get. One parent now has to do the work of two, and this can be very hard. The parent may then ask the children for help, and it is very important for them to try to give this help. Helping your remaining parent makes the parent love you more because you are making life less difficult for him or her. Also, it can make you like yourself more. Doing these extra things can make you feel older, smarter, and more responsible—all very good and worthwhile feelings to have.

Younger children can certainly make beds, fold

clothing that has been washed, pick up and put away things that may have been left around the house, wipe dishes, and do many other useful things in the house.

Older children can cook, sew, do repairs, wash cars, vacuum the carpets, take care of the lawn, and help care for younger children.

Sometimes doing these things can be a lot of fun, especially when everybody joins in and works together as a team. Other times you may not be in the mood to do chores and even be angry that you have to. But even when you may not want to do some of these things, it is good to learn to do them anyway. There are times in life when you have to do things you may not like doing. After you've done them, you may feel good about yourself because of what you have accomplished.

5

SOME IMPORTANT THINGS TO REMEMBER

Children who live in a home in which a parent has died are sometimes jealous of children who have two parents who are living. They feel angry about the fact that one of their parents has died. They think that a dirty trick has been played on them. These are normal feelings to have, and there is nothing wrong with having them once in a while.

Some children may also believe that children with two live parents are *better* than they are. I think this is a foolish and wrong idea. The other children may be *luckier* than the child who has lost a parent, but not better. The parent who has died has had the worst possible luck, and the children who have been left behind have also had very bad luck. But this has nothing to do with their being better or worse than anyone else, just less lucky. Probably the best way to get rid of these jealous feelings is to spend more time with substitutes. Then there will not be as big a difference between what others have and what you have.

Before closing this chapter, I would like to say one very important thing. Life is the most valuable thing we have. It is our greatest treasure. No matter what one believes happens after death, no matter what one's religion teaches about that, just about everyone agrees that it is important to try to make the best kind of life that one possibly can.

Realizing that someday one is going to die can help a person become more appreciative of life, more loving of it, and more aware of how precious it is. If one of your parents has died, it can help you appreciate even better how precious life is and how important it is not to waste it. This is one of the most important lessons one can learn, and the death of a parent can help a child learn it. So the death of a parent, although one of the most terrible things that can happen to you, can still do you some good. It can help remind you to do everything possible not to waste the one life we have— our greatest gift.

ABOUT THE AUTHOR

RICHARD A. GARDNER, M.D., a practicing child psychiatrist and adult psychoanalyst, is Clinical Professor of Child Psychiatry at the College of Physicians and Surgeons, Columbia University, and is a faculty member of The William A. White Psychoanalytic Institute. In addition, he serves as Visiting Professor of Child Psychiatry at the University of Louvain in Belgium. He has written extensively for children, parents and professionals in the field of child psychiatry where he is recognized as one of the leading innovators in the field. His *Mutual Storytelling Technique* and his *Talking, Feeling, and Doing Game* have become standard instruments in child psychotherapy.

Dr. Gardner is certified in psychiatry and child psychiatry by the American Board of Psychiatry and Neurology. He is a Fellow of the American Psychiatric Association, the American Academy of Child Psychiatry, and the American Academy of Psychoanalysis.

Special Offer
Buy a Bantam Book
for only 50¢.

Now you can have an up-to-date listing of Bantam's
hundreds of titles plus take advantage of our unique
and exciting bonus book offer. A special offer which
gives you the opportunity to purchase a Bantam
book for only 50¢. Here's how!

By ordering any five books at the regular price per
order, you can also choose any other single book
listed (up to a $4.95 value) for just 50¢. Some restric-
tions do apply, but for further details why not send
for Bantam's listing of titles today!

Just send us your name and address and we will
send you a catalog!

BANTAM BOOKS, INC.
P.O. Box 1006, South Holland, Ill. 60473

Mr./Mrs./Miss/Ms. _____
(please print)

Address _____

City _____ State _____ Zip _____

FC(A)—11/85

Please allow four to six weeks for delivery. This offer expires 5/86.